Somebody Always Singing You

kaylynn sullivan twotrees

Somebody Always Singing You

university press of mississippi   jackson

The paper in this book meets the guidelines for permanence
and durability of the Committee on Production Guidelines
for Book Longevity of the Council on Library Resources.

Library of Congress Cataloging-in-Publication Data
TwoTrees, Kaylynn Sullivan.
Somebody always singing you / Kaylynn Sullivan TwoTrees.
p. cm.
ISBN 0-87805-981-4 (alk. paper)
1. TwoTrees, Kaylynn Sullivan.
2. Teton Indians—Mixed descent—Biography.
3. Afro-Americans—Biography.
4. Racially mixed people—United States—Biography.
I. Title.
E99.T34A4   1997
973'.04043—dc21
[B]   96-44080
                                                          CIP

00 99 98 97   4 3 2 1

Illustrations by Gail Della-Piana
Designed by Amanda K. Lucas

To Tod

contents

BEING

chapter one
Ihanbla / *to dream*   3

chapter two
Hinhan Tanka / *great owl*   27

chapter three
Anakihme / *secret*   39

chapter four
Pehin / *hair*   50

BECOMING

chapter five
Wokiksuye / *live and remember*   65

chapter six
Iyeska / *mixed blood, interpreter*   101

chapter seven
Cangleska Wakan / *sacred hoop*   122

chapter eight
Dancing between the Worlds   132

BEING

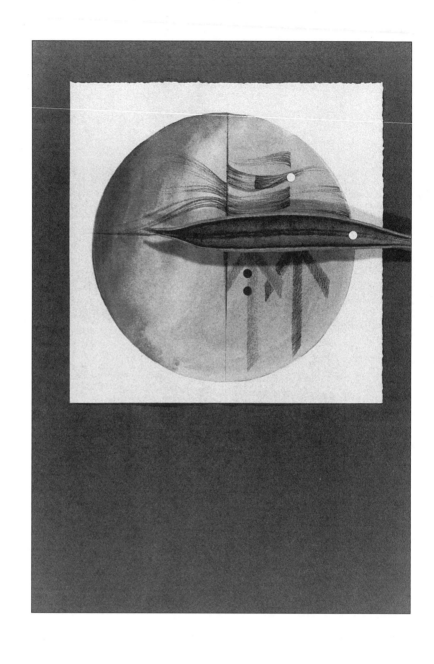

Ihanbla /*to dream*

My grandmother thought I remembered everything she did, even the mem-ories that were not ours. She wove the fragments of things she heard from my father before my birth into the fabric of her own dreaming. I added glimpses given by my mother and father when, in rare moments, they spoke of each other. So a story was born of their meeting and of my birth which suited the needs of each of us.

His mother, Mabel, sent a message to him. He didn't know who had written it for her and taken it to the post office. It said simply: "Your halfside is coming. I dreamt my grandchild, a girl baby. Hinhan Tanka." Only a vision would cause her to go through so much trouble to send him a message.

He touched the letter in his pocket as he watched his reflection in his shoes. The smell of shoe polish still lingered in his nose. From where he stood the reflection looked neat and strong. He looked like a soldier—a sergeant. It made him feel like a warrior. It was this feeling that his father had revealed to him in his youth, and after boarding school he tried to regain it in the army.

The sun was bright, and he could smell the plants waking up to the warmth of the sun and the arrival of summer on the heels of spring.

The smell was green and lush. His eyes took in the ivory magnolias in bloom, while his body soaked up the smell of new grass and the sound of children's laughter. He wanted to smile, but there was always a creeping discomfort when he remembered he was in Georgia. Fort Benning was an army base and he was a sergeant, but it was 1944, this was the South and his skin was brown.

He answered an absentminded hello to someone who yelled "Hi, Art" across the grass. But he kept his eyes lowered on his shoes, not thinking where his feet were taking him. He was pleased with himself. The smells and sounds receded into the background as he let himself think about *her*, the librarian. He had been wondering about her more each time they crossed paths, about the way she held her head and eyes in a veil of sadness, or maybe it was loneliness. He couldn't tell.

The librarian, Daisy, looked out the windows at a sunny and clear day, thinking about a special spot she had found where she could sit undisturbed at lunch time. Today she was missing the Iowa skies. She had thought that the army would be a place for some adventure and learning. Pop had told her there were more opportunities for Negroes who had been in the service, but she hadn't counted on the loneliness and homesickness.

She was waiting for lunch as an opportunity to be alone and read. She was just about to leave when she saw him come into the library. As he pulled open the door, the breeze brought the smell of earth and sky in with him. She knew who he was, but she didn't know his name. He had not been in the library before, but she had seen him several times with some of the men her brother, Junior, visited when he came on leave to see her. It was strange for them to take to an Indian, but they said he was a good man. They teased him for being too quiet and for not dancing. At home anyone who didn't dance was suspect. He had tired of the teasing, and at a party the last time Junior visited he had done one of his own dances. Daisy had been struck by the power of it, and the men didn't talk about dancing anymore.

She lowered her eyes as he came forward so that he wouldn't know she was watching him. He was tall, over six feet, and his hair was glistening black and freshly cut. His eyes were so dark and penetrating that she was afraid to raise hers to them. She could feel his gaze, so she looked away. It was the first time she had experienced her body's awareness of another person. The size of him made her short of breath. He was big, not heavy or fat, but solid and square-shouldered. She smiled to herself at the fact that they were the same color. "So much for red and black races," she thought, as she wondered what he was doing here.

He hadn't realized he was walking into the library until he was there. He tried to think of what he could say, while his feet kept walking towards her. The white duty officer stared at him openly, seeming to question his being there. That wasn't unusual. It always surprised whites when anyone of color used the library, as though they were not expected to read. The officer also watched the librarian. It hadn't occurred to Art that she might have the same hassles in the army that he and the other Negro and Indian men had. He had thought that somehow her education and position as librarian might shield her.

Now all of his energy was focused on her. She was so tiny. She couldn't be more than five feet tall and a hundred pounds. She seemed like a small fragile bird. He saw her eyes filled with that melancholy he had always noticed. It was like a mist around her. He could tell she was watching him even though her head was bent. He liked that. The subtleness of her look reminded him of Lakota women back home.

When he reached the counter where she was standing, the officer was next to her. They said, "May I help you?" at the same time.

He looked at her and spoke to the officer. "I came to take Miss Brown to lunch. We had an appointment." He was shocked at himself. He had never spoken to her before. He knew she was Junior's sister so he had known her name. He certainly expected her to protest. He held his breath. She didn't know him.

But he could see her begin to smile. Her head still bowed, she answered, "You're early. Why don't you have a seat and I'll be ready in a few minutes."

He sat at one of the reader tables and waited. He was not feeling as neat and perfect as he had been. The officer was irritated and gave a few added tasks just to exercise power and cut their lunch short. Art was still numbed by the boldness of what he had done. He remembered his mother's dreaming and the letter in his pocket. He berated himself for having thoughts about a woman he had not even properly met, but the dream kept pulling at the corners of his mind.

He was so engrossed in his feelings of embarrassment and in questions about his mother's letter that he had not noticed her standing in front of him.

"Want to share my lunch?" she asked, holding a brown bag in her hand. He had not thought about food or the fact that he had invited her to lunch, but here she was offering him hers. "I have a special place out back where I eat when the weather is nice. I stay inside too much at this job, and it makes me homesick. Iowa is so open. I don't even know your name."

"Art." He was embarrassed again by her simplicity and honesty. There was a pause, neither of them knowing what to do next. "I'm from South Dakota and I miss the skies and prairies, too." They had begun to walk. They moved out into the breezes and the smell of spring. Sunlight seemed to lift her sadness and make her eyes shine. She was leading the way.

"My name is Daisy. Your name tag says Jones. That doesn't sound like an Indian name."

He watched her smooth her skirt and take off her jacket, then sit on the grass. "Boarding school. Indian name doesn't sound civilized."

She opened the bag and handed him half of a sandwich wrapped in waxed paper. "Why did you say you had an appointment?"

The answer came before he could think, "Because I didn't want to say that I had come to find my halfside." They were both quieted by the words. He was shocked that he had said them, and she was not sure what they meant.

She had never heard anyone talk like that before. She was carried back to her childhood, when she had run through cornfields and hidden in hollow logs with the smell of moss in her nostrils. She wasn't sure why she thought of those things when he talked, and it made her a little afraid.

She found the nerve to look into his eyes, and her fears lifted. She didn't know what "halfside" was, but the breath of the words coming out of his mouth made her feel wanted. She watched him eat his sandwich. First he took a little piece of it, held it up in the air, and gave it to the birds. It was a moment before she realized he had been offering it to the four directions. He waited while the birds ate before he began. Her family didn't say grace before meals very often but she knew that was what he had done.

While they ate he told her about South Dakota—about Pine Ridge, the reservation where he had grown up, and about the places where he had played when he was small. As he spoke, she could feel the expanse of the sky, smell the wind in the grasses and see the bitter stark winters. It was like being on a swing. When he paused and left a silence between them so she could speak, she told him about Gravity, the town where her family had begun their life in the North. He watched the words tumble out of her mouth but was hearing only the music of her voice and seeing the beauty of her eyes as they sparkled deep brown in the sunlight.

When lunch was over, he said simply, "What time?" She knew she would be spending this evening and many others with him.

The certainty that he had found her, his halfside, grew in him as they spent more and more time together. As the waves of her unexplainable fears rose and fell, he soothed her. The differences between them disturbed her and drew her in at the same time. He talked to her about his people, for if she knew who and where he came from, then she would know him and trust the love in his heart. He did not know much about her people, but he knew they had suffered on this land as his own had. There was strong medicine in her family even though it was hidden behind books and words. He felt it. How else could she have come to the dreams of his mother?

She was skittish. She had heard rumors that he was a lady's man. Why had he chosen her? She had never felt pretty, and her family and friends always teased her for being too serious. They called her a bookworm, but Art always looked at her as if she were beautiful. He was so gentle and kind, but she didn't understand the landscape of his thoughts sometimes. The "halfside" idea was beginning to spook her. It seemed to involve more than just being a girlfriend. He was courting her in a way that included his whole family, his whole tribe. It felt like a burden to her, even though in her heart she wanted to be courted, to be loved.

Two months after they began seeing each other, her birthday arrived. It was July, the middle of summer, hot and humid; plants and flowers tumbled over each other in their bursting growth. The air was full of water. At mail call in the barracks she was so excited about the packages she received from home that she had marked them with sweat before she could even get them open. Everyone knew it was her birthday, and the fact that there was already a crowd gathered around her was testimony to her mom's legendary baking skills. She opened the boxes, and the sweet smell of cookies seeped out and crawled along the air that was moved by overhead fans. She and her friends sat around her bunk and had cookies for lunch. The cake her mom had enclosed she was saving for Art.

In the evening he came to celebrate with her. They walked to a grassy place they had found among the trees away from the eyes and noise of people. He began telling her stories again. It was a clear night, and the moon was their candlelight. Only crickets and starlight surrounded them as they laid out the star quilt made by his grandmother. Their bodies touched in the middle of the star, as the white in the quilt reflected the moonlight. Their hands were sweaty, but they didn't let go of each other. They lay very still. He reached into his shirt pocket with his free hand and placed something on her chest.

There were many things she could imagine him giving her as her hand reached out, heavy with expectation. But what she felt was leather, old and worn and formed to the shape of whatever was inside it. Fearful of looking at it, she was also disappointed, but she hid this in movement as she rolled over on her stomach and held it to the moonlight. It looked like a necklace with a small pouch at the end of it. The pouch was beaded, and even with only moonlight she could see that the beads had a patina of wear. The sweat and oil of the body was ingrained in the pattern of the beads.

His voice came out of the night as if it were bringing the past with it. "In the moon when all things ripen, I was born. The string that connected the life of my mother to me was cut so that I would remain on the Earthwalk. My grandmother cut it and made a pouch for it and placed it around my neck for my safety. I wore this until the time when the Indian agent came to tell my parents I had to go to boarding school. My grandmother told my father it was time to take me, hide me and teach me to be a Lakota man before the white man taught me his ways. She took the baby pouch from my neck and buried it. My father and I went away through two moons until the time of quilling and beading, which you call October. We spent time alone together. With him in those days and nights I learned to see and hear with my heart, and I came into my name, *sunkmanitu cekpaku*, Twin Wolf. He helped me take those things which gave strength to my name and to make a pouch for them. To know me and the heart of me I wanted you to hold this pouch near your heart."

Then he reached back into his pocket and brought out a pearly white pouch, newly beaded in the colors she now knew belonged to the four directions. The delicacy of the pouch and the beadwork touched her heart as he placed it around her neck.

"I have taken half of the medicine of my pouch and made a new one for you so that *sunkmanitu* will care for you as half of me."

She began crying both because she was frightened by the strength of his passion and love for her, and because she was disappointed and did not understand this gift. He held her close to his chest and rolled with her onto the grass so that her tears would fall into the hair of Mother Earth. He touched the pouch to her heart.

"What does it mean?" she asked.

He looked at her and smiled. "It means you are part of me."

It wasn't quite the answer she needed to quiet her fears and doubts. His love seemed to ask so much of her.

After he took her home, she sat up most of the night with her best friend, Libby. She couldn't stop crying. In the mist of her tears were all the years she had spent in school, lonely and sad, mixed with all the stories he had told her that calmed her heart but provoked her intellectual skepticism. She cried for her past, which was like the plains in Iowa, flat and distant, and for her childhood, which she could only recall through the eyes of her father's dreams for her. She cried for the love she felt for this man she could not understand. Most of all she cried for herself, because she did not believe she was strong enough to carry what he was entrusting to her. But all of her tears could not match the love growing inside her.

They spent the following days of summer finding places where they could go barefoot in the grass. In this land of infinite layers of green, they learned new names for the flowers and weeds they discovered. In the heaviness of the moisture-laden air, their spirits soared with excitement, love, discovery and the bursting smells of summer. They had been seeing each other at every available moment every day since they met, so, when he was called off on a training assignment, she was glad for the break, for time to be alone and think.

In the stillness of the August air she lay on her bunk daydreaming. She remembered Iowa and the creaking of the porch swing, which made her see flashes of Art sneaking up on a rabbit on one of their walks. She hadn't believed anyone could get that close. She thought about Uncle Lonnie back home and about going rabbit hunting with him. They never got that close. She would walk behind him as quietly as she could, but, when she saw a rabbit, even her looking at it seemed to make noise. These memories floated on the creaking swing song. She closed her eyes till she could see only slits of sunlight and the shapes behind her eyes.

All the memories from home were woven together by the sound of her father's praise and the weight of his ambitions for her. His voice was always there. "Gal, we're so proud of you. Can't wait for you to get home. There are more and more jobs opening up here for us folks. Joe Hamilton is in law school and the Howard boy got some kind of government work."

Her eyes flew open at the words, for she could almost see Burton, Sr., standing right there in front of her, tall and straight, like an apparition. Her father had never been weak. He could always do whatever it took to get his family what they needed. His love for education and reading was the unfulfilled passion of a seeker of knowledge denied opportunity by the times and the responsibilities of family. As the son left at home, he had quit school after the fourth grade to begin barbering. He read constantly and could recite Walter Scott's "Lady of the Lake" or "The Rubáiyát of Omar Khayyám" in their entirety. His greatest happiness came from his daughter's pursuit of her career and his sister's degree in history.

As his image faded she wondered what he would think about a man who lived on an Indian reservation and who answered questions with fables.

By late August the heat and humidity were unbearable. The only thing moving was the ceiling fan in the library. The door was propped open in the hope that a breeze would grace the room. No one was using the library, and the officer had left Daisy in charge of the emptiness.

She was drifting on the pages of a novel, lost in the spider web of words and images, when the stillness was shredded by Libby rushing into the room, breathless and sweating.

"Art has been injured. They brought him to sick bay a few minutes ago." Daisy couldn't make her eyes focus on Libby. She knew that she began to run, but there were no messages going between her brain and her legs. She couldn't even see where she was going, but she knew she had to get to him.

The infirmary was a white world and he seemed small in it, engulfed in pale sheets. All the other beds were empty, neat and perfectly lined up, like soldiers for inspection. She touched the pouch, which she wore around her neck under her uniform, as if it could connect her to him in this world and make its starkness less frightening. His body was not relaxed as she knew it to be when they lay on his grandmother's quilt. It was limp, in an unnatural sleep brought on by drugs and surrender to this sterile place. She put her hand on his chest near his heart. She needed to know that he was real, that he was breathing. On her way in, a nurse had told her that he had been accidentally stabbed in the ribs with a bayonet during a drill, but that the wound was not serious. She still wasn't sure.

"*Mitawicukin,*" he said, with his eyes closed. He took her hand. She didn't know what to say. She had heard enough of his language to recognize that this was Lakota, but she thought he might be delirious. He opened his eyes and looked so deeply into hers that she could not drop her head or turn away.

"*Mitawicukin,* my wife," he said. "I want you to be my wife, my halfside." In a rush all the doubts that had been plaguing her while he was away came rushing at her like a gust of hot air, taking her breath away. But her lips said, "Yes."

As he recovered they became even more inseparable, and when the stitches were removed they decided to get married. Neither of them knew she was pregnant. They found out two weeks after they were married. He was ecstatic. She was paralyzed. It was September, the moon when wild rice is stored. The air was cooling, and they sat outside the barracks talking about the weather so they wouldn't have to talk about the feeling that filled the air between them like static. Every movement towards her caused a ripple through her body like a snake removing itself from the proximity of touch.

They had finally found housing and could move out of the barracks, but the move, along with the planning of a trip to Iowa when he would meet her family, amplified the tension. He had sent a message home so his mother would know that he had found her and could begin preparations for welcoming her to the family. He had also sent gifts to ask for a name to be dreamt for her. He hadn't told Daisy about the name or the welcoming, but he was pleased with the fruit of his mother's dreaming. Daisy didn't want him to tell anyone about the baby until after they had visited her family. Her shame at the untimeliness could not be overcome by his joy. So he agreed but was sure that his mother already knew.

It was Art's turn to be a little nervous as they boarded the train to Iowa to visit Daisy's family. With the landscape shifting through various families of trees, grasses and clouds outside the windows of the train, she never moved her head from his shoulder or the comfort of his arms, and he relaxed. He was happy, thinking that she was finding joy in their union and the life that was beginning inside her. But for Daisy it was a suspension between the strain of keeping her pregnancy secret on the base and her worry about the opinion her family would have of Art. In the movement of the train, the being between places, she was free to love him and the child. For these hours she rode on the motion of his passion and her own sense of life. Only when the train stopped in Des Moines did the creeping dampness of worry cover her skin and seep into her brain and heart. He could feel her body tighten.

It was autumn in Des Moines. The leaves were brilliant gold and red. Her street was lined with maple trees, which made a fiery canopy for them as they drove toward the house in Doc Winter's car. Doc had been a dentist and friend to their family as long as she could remember, and he had picked them up at the train station because her father was still at the barbershop and her mother didn't drive. Art was quiet as Doc and Daisy caught up on neighborhood gossip, their voices seeming distant, like sounds behind a door. He was trying to digest what he was seeing. He felt as though he were looking at scenery in a movie: tree-lined streets, white frame houses bigger than the tribal office on the reservation, cars neatly parked in driveways at almost every house.

The car stopped. They were in front of a three-story white frame house with a large grassy yard. He waited, thinking their entire *tiospaye*, extended family, must live here. Daisy's mother came out the front and towards the car. No one else appeared. Since Daisy got out to greet and hug her mother, he got out, too, but still looked around for the rest of the family.

As he emerged from the car her mother took him in with her eyes, trying to assess this new son-in-law. He had never been to the home of a Negro family before, but he had imagined that their lives and homes would be similar to his. This house was very different. When they went inside, he noticed the wood stairways and saw that the door was beautiful and natural, oiled and cared for. As they came into the living room, he noted that the carpets were not worn under the weight of many footsteps. The sight of the rooms stretching out before him— living room, dining room, study and kitchen—brought many questions to his eyes and lips. He wondered about the cousins, aunts, uncles, sisters, brothers and grandparents. She saw the questions forming in the air and moved closer to him.

"Where are your relatives?" he asked, as he picked up their suitcases from the vestibule of the house and started inside.

"What relatives?" She was trying to pay attention to his uneasiness and read the look in her mother's eyes at the same time.

"Many relatives must live in a house so large or you would have no need for it." She first felt there was criticism in his remark, but his voice was so clear and childlike that her heart opened. She took his hand off the suitcase and led him into the study. He stared at the walls lined with books. To keep them from being interrupted, she called over her shoulder, "Mom, I'm giving Art the tour. I'll be in to help with supper in a bit." As she began, she realized what she had left out of their talks—her stories, the stories of her people.

"My great-grandparents, Henry and Anna, came to Iowa from Virginia with their master and his family. He gave them some land to farm when he gave them their freedom. Henry and Anna had their own children, but some of the children they raised were children of Anna and the master. The master and his wife had a farm nearby, and all those children grew up together, learning to read and write and work the farms. That farm stayed in our family until my grandmother got sick after her husband died. Pop moved the family to town and worked till he got this house and his own barbershop. He took care of his mother and three sisters and sent one of them all the way through college.

"Our family has been able to read and write since they came from Virginia around the 1860s, and it's still very important to us today. During the depression when all the white people around here were losing their money, Pop took his savings and bought this house. It's got thirteen rooms. Grandma lived with us when she was alive and Aunt Iris and Aunt Georgia lived here while they were working and going to school, but they moved away. The Mitchells lived here with their twins when their house burned down. My aunt Gladys lived here while she was studying to be a nurse. But now there is only Mom and Pop waiting for some grandchildren to liven this house up again."

She looked in his eyes and smiled when she said this. He smiled back. She had spoken of their child with joy for the first time. His heart was full. She took out the family picture album and showed him pictures of the family farm and relatives. She felt comfortable sharing this with him in her own home, the house where she knew her baby would play, too.

They walked through the rooms, each one unfolding its story through her so that it sang with the memories of the relatives who had slept and laughed and eaten here. The care he saw in the wood on the stairs represented the work and love of the hands of her parents. They had scraped away the layers of facade and brought the house back to life for their family. All the varnish and coatings, all the wallpaper and linoleum had been scraped away until the wood was revealed and sanded and oiled back to life. He felt *maka unci*, Grandmother Earth, here along with Daisy's family. The house did not seem too big now.

She took him to the back porch so that he could see the trees and yard while she had a chance to talk to her mother under the guise of fixing dinner.

"He's a light-skinned man, Daisy. Are you sure he's an Indian? He could be a mulatto. You never know these days, when our folks are trying to pass for all kinds of things. Have you met his people? When did you meet this nice-looking man? What I want to know is why you didn't tell us you were getting married. You're our only girl and we would have liked to be part of your wedding. What made you be in such a hurry?"

"Love, Mom. Love made us be in such a hurry."

Art came up to the back door, smiling, with Bingo, the dog from next door, by his side. He had his jacket off and his sleeves rolled up. She could tell they had been rolling in the grass and loving it. He came in and walked towards her mother.

The only time the gulf between her people and him was completely gone was that moment in autumn twilight when he walked through the door looking straight into her mother's eyes, holding out his hand, saying, "I am happy to be welcomed into your home and the life of your people."

He gave her mother a strand of braided grass, which she had never seen before. His hand stayed on the braid even when her mother had taken it and placed it near her heart. Their eyes were locked the entire time. Everything in the house was quiet. He had forgotten all the questions he had about her mother's auburn hair and green eyes.

Then a clock buzzed. "Time to put the bread in the oven," her mother said, bringing them back into step from that moment out of time. The kitchen was in motion again. She hung the braid on a hook in the kitchen and got the bread that had been rising in the pantry. Daisy peeled potatoes, and Art went back outside to keep company with the dog until dinner.

Her mother had spent years perfecting her timing. The dining room table was set and the serving dishes heating on top of the stove when Daisy's father drove into the driveway. Daisy knew dinner was close, so she had already called Art to come in and wash up. They were both waiting at the kitchen door as her father came in, hung up his hat, put down his lunch bag and downed the shot of bourbon that was waiting for him on the kitchen table. Then he looked up and saw Art and Daisy with their arms around each other.

"So these are the lovebirds who couldn't wait to get hitched. Glad to meet you, son." He walked over with an outstretched hand, saying, "If you're good to Daisy we'll have no cause to fight." He smiled at Daisy. "Good to have you home, gal." Then he walked off to get ready for dinner.

Art watched him walk away. His back was straight; his strength and pride were visible in his back and the tilt of his head. There were elders back home whose presence had the same power.

He looked at the linen tablecloth and napkins and felt again as if he were in a movie. When they were all seated, Burton said grace, which surprised Daisy. Art felt honored by the richness of the meal and the quantity of meat. It made him think of the welcoming Daisy would receive when she went home with him.

"Have you told your family about the marriage?" Her mother began trying to fill the uneasy silences. Art never spoke unless he felt he had something meaningful to say. He didn't make polite talk just to fill up space, and Daisy hadn't noticed that until now.

He explained having sent a letter to the LameHorse family when they were married. "My mother lives pretty far from the post office and she can't read. So they'll read it to her when they take her out some groceries or supplies."

They had never heard names like TwoTrees and LameHorse except in westerns, and the idea that their daughter's in-laws were illiterate did not sit well. He could sense their disapproval, and he resented feeling as if he had to defend a family of warriors. He thought they might feel differently if they knew something of reservation life.

"Living that far from the BIA, the Indian agent's office, can be a blessing sometimes. My grandmother and my dad taught me a lot about the ceremonies and about our own language before I got taken off to boarding school to learn English. We were not allowed to speak our language there, so I am glad I learned before then and could remember things and talk to the elders."

It reminded Daisy of the stories about the slaves trying to keep their language, beliefs and music alive behind the master's back. She tried to make these comparisons part of the dinner conversation, but Burton wanted to know Art's intentions for the future: where they would live, what his profession was, and what their plans were. Art answered in the way he answered Daisy, sometimes with the stories of his people and sometimes with concrete ideas. Burton voiced his concerns point-blank. "You can't mean to take Daisy to an Indian reservation. Things are tough enough for Negroes without getting involved in Indian ways."

Art looked at Daisy and thought about their child and knew these ways were already connected. He didn't say anything. It was not good to speak in anger to your elders, and he was hurt by Burton's words.

Uncle Lonnie's arrival the next day created a truce in which they could reside without questions. He came in with a couple of raccoons and a possum he had hunted the day before. Art offered to join in skinning and cleaning the raccoons and told Gladys one of his mother's recipes. He told Lonnie that possums dig among the dead, and that he didn't feel good eating them. Lonnie said he would take the possum home, but he was glad to have help anyway. Normally Daisy's parents would have discouraged Lonnie from leaving his catch, but now they needed for something to occupy Art while they talked to Daisy about what she had done.

Art and Lonnie took their knives and the animals out back. Lonnie's hands were cracked and weathered from working outside without gloves. Although it was sunny, the air was cold and their hands stiffened quickly as they met the blood of the animals. They worked on the ground, their hands moving quietly in acknowledgment of each other's adeptness at the job. They were at ease with the work and with each other. As they worked Art broke the silence with songs and words in Lakota. Lonnie couldn't understand the words, but he kept hearing one word over and over again: *tunkashila*. He knew Art was doing some kind of praying. He had hunted with Blue, an Ojibwa friend from the lake country, who always prayed for the hunt, the killing and the cleaning. It felt good to pray over the animals that would feed you, and it was good to be out in the sun doing this work with someone who appreciated it. His sister, Gladys, had gotten too citified. She always acted like this wasn't good honest food. He asked Art about the words while they were cutting up the meat for stew.

"The animals are our relatives, and when they give their lives so that we may eat and live, then we pray to the creator, our grandfather, *tunkashila*, in thanksgiving." Lonnie knew that was a good thing. Art and Blue might seem strange to some, but they had an understanding of life. These animals he hunted were his only meat. He didn't believe in butcher shops. Lonnie thought, "Daisy got herself a good man."

While Lonnie and Art worked through the afternoon sun, Gladys and Burton sat with Daisy in the kitchen. Around the kitchen table with coffee cups filled, under the braid of sweetgrass and a "God Bless This House" plaque, they both had hard questions for her. Burton kept asking, "Where will you live? Your time is almost up in the service, and you can't be thinking about going to live on an Indian reservation."

She had always thought they would come to Iowa and live near her parents, but she realized they had never talked about it. She told them that she wanted to meet his mother, but they were adamant in their disapproval of a trip to the reservation. Gladys asked, "Are you sure he wants to come here and live?" Nothing else had even occurred to her. She had plans for a degree in library science and hoped to get a job then either in the library or at the university. She wasn't sure what he would do. He was a machinist in the army and could find decent work here, but he hadn't talked about his plans. She remembered now that she hadn't asked.

The questions formed around her like an ambush, and she wondered what else they would say if they knew she was pregnant.

Piercing this thought, her mother's question struck her like a bullet. "What about your children? Would you take them to a reservation where their family couldn't read or write? What kind of example is that? Negroes like us have worked hard to pull ourselves out of slavery and make a place for ourselves in this white man's world. I scrubbed floors in places where I couldn't even go to the bathroom, and Dad started cutting hair at twelve years old so our family, you and Junior, could go to school."

She wondered if they had dreams of their own, for themselves, if they had secret desires. She had heard this litany before and usually shrugged it off because she felt she was doing the right thing. Now the weight of it stifled her, as if her future were the only dream they had, and nothing she could do would fulfill it. Besides that, the idea of living on the reservation scared her, even the idea of a visit. She wondered if Art thought they would live there.

Before they could go any further, the side door swung open with a draft of cold air and the smell of freshly butchered meat. Art helped Gladys with the recipe. They didn't talk much in the kitchen, but Art told a few stories about his mother and her life at Pine Ridge. Dinner eased the conversation into neutral territory: hunting, fishing and the weather. Besides, they were leaving the next morning.

The good-byes at the train station were formal, and everyone was glad for departure time. As Art and Daisy got on the train and settled in for the return to the base, he hoped they would find the same closeness they had had on the trip there, but the uneasiness of the visit lingered, tinged with anger. The trees were losing leaves, and some of his joy was leaving, too. His love for her grew and deepened each day, but he was unable to remove the sadness in her heart. He watched her stare out the window. "Are you dreaming for our child?" he asked.

The question made her words burst out in anger. "No, I'm worried about our child's future."

He ignored her anger and began to talk to her quietly about home and the evening skies and morning sunrises. "You are Lakota now. You are my halfside. You will be received into our family and in time given a name. Our family will share food and gifts so that everyone will know we are thankful. Our baby will blessed. My mother dreamt this child. She will honor you and prepare for its birth. You must find peace so that the child enters the Earthwalk in peace and happiness."

It was the first time he had seen anything like real anger come from her. "I am not Lakota. I am a Negro. I am your halfside, your wife, but I am also me. My family comes from slavery. My aunts remember stories of slavery from their grandmother. My grandmother has the bill of sale for her own mother. It is a reminder of how far we have come. Our medicine is reading and writing. This has opened the doors of the future for our family, and it has even brought you and me together. I loved school and the world that I saw through books. So I am afraid for our child. I am afraid of the dreaming of your mother that I do not understand. It is not even dreaming in my own language. I do not know how to be your halfside and to be myself. And I do not know what our child will be."

Her anger faded into tears, and he could think of nothing to say. He was wounded by her words. As the train moved on and she stared out the window, he sang to the child inside her.

Their love never diminished, but the questions in her heart and from her parents, together with the realities of day-to-day living, made a crack in their marriage. And his sadness grew as the baby grew inside her. She had found reasons not to go home with him, and it hurt him deeply. First she claimed that the South Dakota weather would be too hard in her pregnancy. He thought of his aunts bundled in buffalo robes, with babies swelling their bodies, and the wind slicing through the landscape. It was always a good time, waiting for the gift of birth through the dark months. As spring approached he became more hopeful. She was close to the end of her tour, and he could get leave. But she chose to shorten her duty with leave time and go home to her family for the birth. She had not asked him first and did not want to understand how this hurt him. She prepared to leave for Iowa, and he went to Pine Ridge on leave alone. It was the moon of ponies shedding hair. She called it May. They traveled to their separate families.

Her parents were thrilled with her decision to come home and have the baby. They had already turned one of the upstairs bedrooms into a nursery. She settled into her old life at home, and they did not mention Art in the hope that she would forget him or that he would come to live like them. They did not actually invest much energy in envisioning the latter, but they wanted Daisy to be happy. She had always been such a sad child, and he seemed to make her smile. So if that was what it took, then they had plenty of room for him here. Burton could even help find him a job.

When Art arrived at Pine Ridge, the South Dakota landscape and his mother's cabin were the same, full of the spirit and love he had hoped to find in Daisy's home. He hadn't minded having to wait for a ride the whole morning. He hadn't even minded the field of mud he had to cross to get to the porch. When he walked onto the porch, scraping his shoes on the side of the concrete block which served as a step, he felt like he was walking into the arms of his truest love. There were two cups on the table, and the coffee was steaming in both of them. His mother had her hands cupped around one of them.

"*Wakalapi hin waste mayelo.* The coffee smells good, Mom." She nodded and smiled and pushed the other cup toward him as he sat down. Her hair was braided, as always, and there were more wrinkles than he remembered. She had on one of the housedresses he had sent her a few Christmases ago and an old sweater that had belonged to his dad. Her elbows came through the sleeves, and there were so many small holes it almost looked like a pattern. He had sent her new sweaters, but she liked feeling close to his dad when she wore this. As they sat across from each other, she took his hand and looked at him, gazing deep into his eyes till he felt her surround him.

He sat there and let the sadness of making this journey alone over-take him and speak to her. He could smell the cedar and sweetgrass recently burned and the coffee still bubbling on the wood stove.

"*Tanyan yahi yelo.* Good for my eyes to see you and your sadness. Your heart breathes here. If the mother will not birth this baby on our land bring the birth cord back to me." She spoke softly to him, and the sound of his own language brought him some peace.

He chopped wood and hauled water from the pump outside every day. He helped with all the things that would make his mother's days easier. Summer was coming, but she still needed wood chopped for the cooking stove. His cousins came and helped to find a fifty-gallon drum, which he rigged outside the house with a hose so she didn't have to haul water every day. It felt good to be working like this.

He knew he had come home for many reasons: to be in the land of his birth, to crawl into the sweatlodge with his family and ask healing for himself and his marriage, to fast in the hills where his father had taught him to listen with his heart. Perhaps he might discover how to make happiness with Daisy. And when these prayers were finished he came to be strengthened by the words of his mother for the birth of his daughter.

When it was the moon of ripened berries and the time of gray light filling the space between night and day, he heard that the baby was coming soon and left South Dakota for Des Moines. Lonnie picked him up at the bus station and told him that Daisy was already in labor. He met Burton and Gladys and asked to go directly to the hospital even though they offered him something to eat. He watched the sky change colors as they drove him there. The maternity ward had been full when Daisy arrived, with room for "coloreds" only in the orthopedic ward, so that's where she was. The family was not allowed to see her right away, because the hospital was trying to find another space for her while she waited for a place to open in the maternity ward. She had been wheeled into the hallway, and he was allowed to be with her for a few minutes.

"This daughter of ours is trying to be born in the power of changing light." He said this as he took her hand and kissed her forehead, wiping the sweat from it. She was irritated by his certainty that it was a girl, as if his knowing were a threat to her, but the pains were so close together now that she couldn't think about that. She called for the nurse, and he was ushered back into the waiting room.

He began thinking about birth at home. He had been born in the cabin he had just left, where his mother still lived. He had watched his brother and nieces and nephews come into the world, prayed over by their families and washed by the grandmothers who had dreamt them. Their cords had been taken in a sacred way to be made into the medicine bundles that would protect them in their youth.

At the hospital he talked to Burton and Gladys about the cord, but their embarrassment at such foreign thinking pushed them to discourage him from speaking to the doctors. As soon as they went for coffee, he found the doctor. The doctor did not pay much attention to him and surely didn't hear his request. He kept walking and answering questions from the nurse while Art was talking. Daisy's parents saw him and apologized to the doctor for Art's rudeness. Their worlds were colliding around this birth at the same time that they were coming together in the child.

He began to sing softly to his daughter to welcome her to this Earthwalk while he waited. Burton and Gladys moved away from him in the waiting room. As the song was ending, a nurse came in and announced that it was a girl. "I know. *Wopila, tunkashila*. Can I see them now?"

She led him down the hall, and he sang again. When the nurse laughed quietly, he trusted her. He told her about the birth cord and what it meant for his daughter and his mother. She listened. She had never met an Indian before, and his concern touched her. She knew hospital policy, especially dealing with "coloreds," and that any deviation could cause a lot of problems.

"You must be kidding. I'd lose my job if they caught me doing something like that." He was singing again, standing over his wife and their daughter. She was still in the hallway. The baby had been born in the corridor, but here she was, full of life and energy. She was squirming inside the blanket, and, looking closer, he could see a tiny red scratch on her cheek.

"She was so feisty," Daisy explained, "when she came out, and they didn't have any mitts for her because we weren't in maternity. Before they could bundle her up she scratched herself on the cheek." Daisy looked tired but peaceful for the first time. He bent over and put his mouth to the scratch on the baby's cheek, then kissed Daisy. "A warrior," he whispered.

Just as he said it the nurse reappeared. She smiled at the three of them. "That scratch will disappear before you know it." She came closer and put something wrapped in cloth in Art's pocket. He touched it and was glad. The sadness was still in Daisy's eyes, and the scratch would grow into a scar that would stay with his daughter all her life, but she was in his mother's care.

The next day they named her Kaylynn. He stayed for a few days longer. The family did not make much room for him, and even the portrait that was taken at his daughter's homecoming was done while he was out hunting with Lonnie. No record of his presence at her birth seemed necessary to Daisy's family. He took the bundle in his pocket home to his mother.

chapter two

Hinhan

Tanka /*great owl*

Hinhan Tanka, Grandmother Mabel, was so sure that I remembered the same things she did that I made a game of unraveling her memories from mine. The years make clear that, in this sorting, I am remembering her memories.

I remember the summer of my sixth birthday. Mom and Dad had been divorced for two years, and, since she had remarried a year earlier, she didn't want me going to South Dakota anymore. I cried for days and talked about nothing else. The trips with my dad were fun, whether we drove or took the bus, and the thought of missing that and of not seeing Grandmother Mabel devastated me. I begged and cried and didn't eat until she finally said I could go if she could find someone else to take me. Aunt Malvina and Uncle Edmund were travelling to Minnesota to go fishing and said they would take me to Rapid City. It was a couple of days before my stepfather agreed, but I knew in my heart that I would see *Unci*, my grandmother, that summer even if I missed seeing my dad. Mom sent a message to my aunt at nearby

Rosebud Reservation asking for someone to meet me in Rapid City. We got a note from Uncle Billy that said, "I'll be there."

Aunt Malvina was my mom's best friend and worked with her at the university library. She was also my godmother, but I didn't know what that meant. She and Uncle Edmund had a good car that was clean inside. A 1950 Dodge, it was green and cream with soft green upholstery, and I wasn't allowed to have food in the car because I might get it dirty. When we were hungry we would find a place by the side of the road, off where no one could bother us, and have a picnic. She had packed all these meals for the trip so we wouldn't have to find restaurants. "Isn't all that friendly along the highways for Negroes," she told me, "and it costs money to eat other people's cooking."

Malvina and Edmund didn't have any children, and they carried on their conversations as if I weren't there. "Daisy is lucky she decided to divorce Art and come on back home. Burton had to spend a lot of time with her talking to her about her future before she got the nerve to call it off. It turned out good though. What could she do on an Indian reservation anyway? Even when they visited Oklahoma she had problems with some of his people. Gladys said Art's mother doesn't even read or write and she speaks in some Indian language most of the time." Then she would remember that I was in the car. "You know, baby, you're lucky to be with your mom and her family. They've been educated for a long time and they've helped a lot of our folks get ahead. Besides, your stepdaddy is a good man. He's got his own business and his family is nearby."

I couldn't say what I felt about this man who wanted me to call him Daddy, but I had to object a little. "PawPaw says he's crazy, and he and Mom fight and yell a lot."

"Your grandpa says things he doesn't mean sometimes. Besides, married people fight sometimes, don't they, Edmund?" We were driving to Sioux City and the sky opened up and filled my eyes. I drifted on the expanse. The further into the open skies we went, the better I felt.

Their voices became a hum in the background. I could hear snatches of their conversation as they compared "our folks" to Indians when we passed through places where we were unwelcome.

The longer we were in the car, the more comments they made about having to take me to Rapid City. Edmund usually started. "If we didn't have to go to Rapid City we could stop off and see cousin Betty."

Malvina would add fuel to this. "You know if we had been driving alone we could have driven straight up to the lake." I wondered why they had offered to make the side trip. But it didn't matter. I was going to see *Unci*.

When we got to Rapid City, Uncle Billy was waiting for us in front of the diner across from the bus station. He was leaning against the open door of his old pickup, wearing jeans, a worn shirt, a beaded belt buckle, and a cowboy hat to shade his eyes from the South Dakota sun. I was home. I opened the door, ran out and jumped into the pickup on his side. He went over, tipped his hat to Malvina and Edmund and took my suitcase out of the car. When he called to me to say "good-bye," I turned my head a little and flung the "bye" over my shoulder. He hoisted the suitcase into the back of the truck and got in. On the way to *Unci*'s he didn't talk about them. Uncle Billy's name was Redhawk, and he talked about the *cetan*, the hawk. He let me sit very close all the way to Grandmother Mabel's.

When we got near the house, the dirt road and the dusty bare yard merged into one another amidst the patches of grasses. The yard revealed itself by the absence of grass, which had all been worn away by animals, children and feet at work. The chickens lived in a small wire enclosure to the side of the house. Grandmother Mabel had a rooster and two hens. One summer there were six or seven hens, but hunting wasn't so good so we had gotten back down to two again. *Unci* said the rooster liked to have a choice. Four rabbit hutches were left from the time when she had had some tame rabbits; now she stored old jars in them.

Grandmother Mabel didn't drive, so there were no broken cars in her yard. But there were a couple of washing tubs, an old icebox and the big tub we bathed in. The door to the icebox stood ajar, letting light shine on the sacks of dried corn and seed and grain for the chickens. It was closed up tight at night to keep out the other critters. The door to the ice compartment was shut to protect the meats that had been dried or smoked.

On the side of the house opposite to the chicken coop, a groove was worn from the front step of the porch around the side of the house to the outhouse. There was no attempt at design. A slant-roofed outhouse like most others, it was covered with things *Unci* found on her walks. She'd bring back bottle caps and nail them on. She had made a medicine wheel of them. She had also flattened rusty cans to cover holes in the wood, and barrel hoops were draped around like necklaces. In each trip to the outhouse I'd see something I hadn't noticed before.

The step up to the front porch was a cinder block that was half buried in the ground from the years of being walked on. My dad had filled in the space under the porch with concrete so that it looked like some kind of foundation. It kept the winter winds from taking hold underneath and gave the house a feeling of permanence.

The cabin had been built by my grandfather. It was slab board and planks. The porch was plank, supported by trees that hadn't been stripped. The bark was still holding on in some places, and my favorite pastime was to find places to peel it off when I was bored. As parts of the house fell prey to the wind and cold, slab wood was nailed on as a second layer secured with scavenged boards.

Inside was slab wood with plank floors. *Unci* was continuously papering the walls with newspaper articles featuring pictures that she liked. That was our connection to the written word, and it was also the background for the gallery of pictures she had of her family. My dad had sent lots of photos from the army, and these covered the wall by her bed. She had only one picture of his brother, Oran, who was killed in a fight in Rapid City before my dad went into the army.

The cabin consisted of one room with a double bed where the children had been sired and born. The bed had a metal frame and a sagging mattress propped up by boards and was always meticulously made, with no wrinkles or creases. Spread over the top was a star quilt in reds and yellows. There were crocheted pillows at the head of the bed, made by nieces and other family members over at Rosebud; folded over the foot of the bed was a Pendleton blanket given to Grandpa for a healing he had done for Bearheart, a Kiowa friend.

Grandmother Mabel had a wooden table and, at the present time, three chairs; the number of chairs had varied over the years. When the boys were at home, the life span of the kitchen chairs was shortened by their leaning on the back legs and riding them like horses. Since the boys had left, chairs stayed around the table for years at a time. The table was covered with a patterned oilcloth that my dad had brought to her on one of his visits home on leave. After each meal she wiped it very carefully. When she worked on the table, peeling potatoes or preparing fruit for canning, she took the cloth off and folded it up on the shelf above the washstand.

There were three windows, two facing the back of the house and one in the front. She said she would rather look out at the sweatlodge and the land of her ancestors than at the dust from pickups on the road. Between the bed and the kitchen table there was an overstuffed chair covered with two blankets. Each blanket had holes, but the second filled in where there were holes in the first. These blankets had belonged to her grandmother and were used to cover whatever chair she sat in to look outside. There was also a footstool covered with a piece of deer hide, and I would sit there at her feet sometimes.

She had a little nightstand with a kerosene lamp by her bed. Above it on the wall was her eagle wing fan, and on the nightstand there were always small pieces of fabric filled with tobacco and tied together in a string, called tobacco ties. A metal suitcase filled with her medicine was stored under the bed.

The corner opposite the bed was called "the kitchen." A wood-burning cookstove stood there, along with a washstand and some wooden shelves. There was also a tank for water, and a pail hung on the wall for carrying it. The floor in this part of the cabin was covered with old license plates which she and Grandpa had collected. They had been nailed into place like tiles and had been scrubbed to the sheen of chrome over the years. The pots and pans hung from ropes or sat holding water on the stove. *Unci* didn't believe in having a lot of anything, and the dishes she had stayed stacked on the washstand.

That day Uncle Billy left right at sunset. *Unci* and I sat in the quiet cabin as the light changed. It was her favorite time of day, and she said we should be still when the light changed. "Spirits like changing light. They come closer and we don't want to scare 'em." She was sitting in her chair by the window. Her gray hair was in two braids, as always, and she had on one of the housedresses Dad bought her. Over it she had an apron sewn together from flour sacks, and cotton stockings were rolled down around her ankles. Her moccasins looked like they had been made on her feet. Her face was creased with wrinkles from sun and weather. I looked above her at the photograph of her and Grandpa. She was young and her face was smooth. She was standing so that her buckskin dress with its quill work yoke was mostly visible. Her two braids lay on her chest with beaded hair ties, and her hand rested on Grandpa's shoulder. He was wearing a suit, but you could see that his braids reached almost to his waist. He looked erect and strong even though he was sitting down. They both looked directly forward, their gaze so intense that they came right into the present.

Summers we spent most of our time outside. There was an old seat on the front porch where *Unci* would settle when the chores were done and there were stories to be told. Each day began at first light when she would go outside and greet the day and the four directions. When I was a baby she would wrap me and take me out with her and lay me on the ground as she prayed. But when I got older she would wake me up; I would follow her outside and stand beside her, learning her song and watching the birds.

Most of the time I would stay away from the sweatlodge, because it was far behind the house. I knew it wasn't a place for playing. But sometimes I would go there and crawl inside the uncovered willow frame and sit for a while or take a nap. I didn't think then that she knew I was back there, but now I'm sure she did. When Uncle Billy came with friends to use the lodge I would see it being covered, the stones being heated and the men going in. I would watch the fire and listen to the singing. When the fire tender carried in the glowing rocks, I could hear the men greet the stone people.

I liked watching them come out of the lodge with their bodies steaming and their heads bowed. I tried to remember some of the songs when I lay in the uncovered lodge. It was a good way to learn about the lodge.

She let me play freely. I didn't have to be in sight for her to know what I was doing and whether or not I needed her. She would get meat ready for smoking or drying, clean fruit for canning, sort beads for the loom, or hand-sew some clothes for me while I made myself busy trying to help. When I couldn't think of anything to do she would pat the floor next to her, and I would sit for her stories while she kept on working. And there were always the daily chores. We fed the chickens and collected eggs before we ate or cleaned the cabin in the morning. Then we made the bed and swept out the dust from the day before. We would both carry water for washing the dishes at the end of the day, for coffee and for wetting down the floor a little so the house wouldn't be so dusty.

She remembered the first time my dad brought me to her. "Not thirteen moons you came to me. *Wipazuka Wasta Wi*, the moon of ripened berries, the moon of your birth, you come home. I feel you come. I wait outside for first look of you, and *niyatekin,* your father, put you on the ground. You come to me and cry. I see you in city clothes. It makes me sad. I give you your own birth medicine so you know you are *Lakota. Wokiksuye.* You live and remember the dreaming from *Unci.*"

The summers were always marked by the clothes I would get when I went to Grandma's. Every time, no matter what my mom sent with me, *Unci* would put the suitcase under the bed alongside the metal suitcase and leave it there all summer. I had a pair of pants she would make and a shirt. I had a buckskin dress which was a little too big for me so I could grow and still wear it, and I had a nightgown made from an old housedress of hers. She traded quill work for fabric from the quilters, and she sewed the clothes by hand. She never sent them back with me. She just folded them up when I left and made a new set when I came back. I was six when I finally grew into the buckskin dress, and she started a new one I would never see.

I remember her taking my hand and leading me to the door on the night of the new moon. We would stand on the porch while the sun set and the shadows would outline everything near the house. Then the dark would swallow everything until our eyes adjusted and the outlines would reemerge. She would take me around back to sit on a bench made from a plank she had set on two stumps. Beyond us we could see the shadow of the sweatlodge. She never let go of my hand till we sat down. She was my guide in the dark and my safety for this game we had together. It took a long time for my eyes to get accustomed to the dark, and my nose would catch whiffs of smoked meat or water lingering in the metal tub. I knew what I was supposed to do. I was to sit as still and be as silent as I could. Sometimes I would even hold my breath because it seemed so loud in the night. I would strain my eyes to see all the things I remembered from the daylight. She would sit next to me holding an old quilt on her lap. We sat like that for a long time, till I could see almost everything. The night animals would start to move closer to the cabin. The raccoons would make forays to the garbage, then run off. The skunks were detectable only by their scent. And sometimes the porcupines would come. When this happened, we would let them get close to us while we sat very still on the bench. Then, in a motion so swift I never could believe she had done it, she would throw the old quilt on the porcupine. A second later she would retrieve it filled with quills. Inside we removed them and the barbs. Later they would be sorted by size for storage in pouches containing already-sorted quills from previous adventures.

We both remembered her trying to teach me the plants. "You listen with half ear. She who hears half, a good name for you." She would rock with laughter. "Bird people talk, pull your mind to the sky. *Waste.* That is good to listen to the bird nation. Good also to listen to earth relatives. You must know your friends from the green when you are sick. We walk and I ask them to teach you. When it is too hot to walk, we sit. I say their names for you in Lakota so they will know you."

I would listen to the names and remember for a summer. They would be clear to me while we were picking flowers and berries to use in dyeing the porcupine quills. But each time I went away from the Black Hills, the words left my head. Some of them still whisper to me, but the names and teaching that came from her are hidden in some inner closet.

I remember the nights when we were waiting for water to boil for my bath; she would sit at the table softening quills in her mouth and decorating birch bark toys. In the hottest days of summer we would build a fire outside and set one of the big pails over it to heat. This was a treat for me, because most days we washed in cold water poured over ourselves for a quick rinse. The ceremony of taking a real bath was one of my favorites. I would spend part of the day helping to fill the big pail, bucket by bucket. She had a bucket and I had a little one, and we would fill them at the pump and carry them to the pail.

Hinhan Tanka / *great owl*   35

While the fire heated she would work on toys that she would send home with me at the end of the summer: dolls, birch bark canoes decorated with quills, and small boxes made of birch bark for holding my secret things. We didn't talk much. *Unci* said the mouth must be still when the hands are learning, and my hands were busy beading on the loom we had built. Sometimes she would sing. When the water was hot we would scoop it with buckets and carry it to the old metal tub we had set in the yard. We would put in buckets of cold water, too. She would test the water with her elbow, and, if it was safe, would have me get undressed. Then I would climb into the water, and she would tell me stories of water, steam and creation while she scrubbed every inch of me.

When the weather was cool we took the metal tub inside, and the pails would heat on the wood stove while the windows steamed up. Our world of stories was sealed in the mist of the bath. It felt safe and warm. As the water cooled and I was ready to get out, she wrapped me in a small quilt she had made for me and dried me by the stove.

Now when I am feeling down or alone, I make a bubble bath for myself. I light candles to remind me of the kerosene lamp, and I pretend I am in *Unci*'s metal tub hearing her voice and feeling her touch.

Some memories were the same for us. It is hard to say what holds these memories in place or what recalls them to us. The summer I was four years old, South Dakota was dusty and dry, and Pine Ridge was even dustier. *Unci* was inside canning berries. The day was filled with the smell of fruit and sugar. I knew we would have meat and *wojapi*, a kind of fruit sauce, for dinner. I was sitting on the porch squinting at the sun so I could see those shapes behind my eyes and continue the stories floating in my head. I heard her call me, and I didn't answer at first. I just started telling the story I was seeing out loud. She sat down beside me until I was finished and held my hand. We sat like that for a while. All you could hear were the flies in the hot midday sun and the sound of old cars on dirt roads in the distance.

She led me back into the house and pulled the metal suitcase from underneath the bed. I was breathless. I had imagined so many things about that suitcase. She sat on the floor and opened it. All I saw was red cloth. Then she took my hand and brought me to her side. She unfolded the cloth and pulled out a large wing. For a moment I saw an owl staring at me with its wings outstretched. Then it was just a wing. I started crying until I heard her voice. She said, "This is a wing from *hinhan tanka*. My name comes from this nation. They share their name and their medicine with me and now with you. *Hinhan tanka* will stay with you."

We spent a long time going through the things in the suitcase. Her voice was a cloud that surrounded me as she brought out bundles, leather pouches, cedar and cornmeal. The smell of the sweetgrass she had lit after opening the suitcase filled the room. We were cloaked in that smell and the softness of her voice. There was one moment, especially, so clear that it has remained with me all these years in its perfection. She was holding a small bundle and she looked at me hard, pointed at me and said, "You, going/coming back being. Don't talk so much coming back. Makes going clear and coming back stronger. Grandmothers always singing you going. Grandchildren always singing you coming back. Somebody always singing you, going/coming back being."

That was my inheritance. She said it to me many times before we were separated, but we both remembered that first time with the same fullness of feeling.

She remembered the owls coming to her the first time and retold it often when she was teaching me the things I needed to learn from the grandmothers. And later, when we were separated, I would retell the story for myself and to keep it alive for my granddaughter.

"I come to this place with the trees for *hinhan tanka* with my halfside. I am young and we make this house together while the berries ripen in our first year. When it is done and we are living and living and living a baby grows inside me. In the full moon of your father's birth the trees call me and I feel *hinhan tanka* but I do not understand their speaking." Here she would take a breath and wait just as she waited for her understanding of the owl nation.

"*Istawicayzan wi*, moon of snow-blind eyes. It is so cold that I do not want to go. I wear our buffalo robe. The moon and snow make the night white. In the trees *hinhan tanka* is waiting. Across the field I can see the eyes. Then I am with them in the trees. My feet are not in moccasins. They hold on the branch like *hinhan tanka*. On the ground I see man and woman with baby. The man takes baby and woman stops. He hold baby to us. Then baby is in the tree. It is a small *hinhan hota*. I begin to feel cold and I am standing in the snow with a feather near my feet. Now I know *hinhan tanka* speaking."

She told me this story often, and when she did she touched the pouch around my neck to remind me that she and *hinhan tanka* were always with me. I kept that pouch until I was seven and went to live with my mother's parents. But the story lives in memory.

chapter three

Anakihme /*secret*

It was my sixth summer, and the trip to South Dakota had been cut short by Mom's demand that I come back to Iowa. She didn't give me or *Unci* a reason, but I saw fear in her eyes when I got home. I missed the dust of Pine Ridge. It was humid, and the air was heavy with music and boredom. Images of South Dakota kept moving across my mind, contrasting the fullness of my summer there with the one I was having in Iowa. The park was filled with the sound of kids amusing themselves in the pool. I could smell the chlorine even though I was up on the deck overlooking the pool. The parking lot was full of cars of teenagers looking to ease their boredom. Across the street, on the porches of frame houses with peeling paint, the old people sat, trying to keep tabs on the activities of the younger generation in the park. And always there was music, from car radios and portable radios at poolside, weaving everything together with rhythm and blues.

The sounds followed me across the street to my house. I was hungry. Most of the other kids had gone off in groups to the corner store or to someone's house. I was left to my own devices. My absence during most of the summers had left me outside the clubs and cliques that formed at the pool or playground. So I didn't have to worry about breaking the rules and bringing kids in the house while Mom and my stepdad, Will, were not at home. This day I climbed up the stairs to the porch thinking about the peanut butter and jelly sandwich I would make, while the sound of double Dutch and a blues guitar followed me like background music. Then I noticed that the front door was open.

I could see through the screen door that Will was sitting there in the big blue armchair. He had moved it from its place next to the couch and the big radio into the middle of the room so that it faced the door. I was surprised to see him. It made me scared. Usually he was still at his print shop this time in the afternoon, and Mom and I would have some time to ourselves before he came home. His presence upset us both in different ways. Seeing him alone made my stomach knot. I wanted to turn back. There was never any comfort in the two of us together. It took Mom to make some kind of balance, and seeing him like this made even the house seem strange.

He was absorbed, working on something. He looked different. Everything looked different. The wallpaper pattern was illuminated so that it was not just background. It was alive and full of light. The looped weave of the upholstery of the chair and couch stood out like a foreground in a still life. It also gave me space to look at Will. He had a box of bullets in his lap. He was working in slow motion, filing the ends of them with a metal file. I had been hunting enough with Uncle Lonnie and Uncle Billy to know that he wanted to hurt something badly. I thought that maybe raccoons were getting in the garbage again at Lonnie's, but that thought did not sit well with me. I went quietly to my room, forgetting the peanut butter and jelly sandwich.

He didn't even look up as I passed him. I closed my door a little when I got inside. Mom and Will never let me keep it closed completely. I stayed quiet and listened to the rustle of the pattern in the wallpaper. I wanted to go out, to call someone, but I was afraid to walk past him again. Just as small animals understand the change in wind and scent to mean the coming of danger, I knew the chair being moved and the sounds in the wallpaper meant danger for us.

I stayed in my room as it got darker. I heard him get up and turn on the porch light, but I could see no lights in the living room. I didn't turn on the light in my room. I didn't want to be noticed. The changing light made me miss the smell of dinner coming through the house. It felt and smelled empty and cold, even in the August heat, and I fell asleep to the sound of his metal file on the bullets.

I was awakened by the sound of Mom's footsteps on the porch, and I wanted to run out and hug her, but I crawled to the doorway to see if Will was still sitting there. I stopped by the door. The air stopped, too. There was a pause as she put her hand to the screen door and peered inside. Everything unrolled in slow motion. Opening the door, she was smiling at Will, her mouth open, about to say something. I was afraid to look at him so I kept my eyes on Mom.

Her face changed as the open door let the porch light illuminate where he was sitting in the room. Her mouth never closed. It changed from a smile to a scream that was never heard. The screen door slammed behind her as the first bullet ripped into her throat and threw her backwards. Blood flew around the room like a storm wind. The second bullet somehow ricocheted so that it knocked out the porch light. Before it did I could see her body lifted and slammed back against the closed screen door. There was a hole ripped through the screen. The wallpaper's pattern was blurred with blood. There was so much blood that I could feel it on my clothes, and my nose was filled with its warm metallic smell.

After the first shot I could see Mom reaching out for help. She couldn't make a sound. There was only blood and ripped flesh where her chest and throat had been. The white blouse she had on framed the wound as if it were a painting. After the second shot she was still. Her body looked smaller. Everything was blood. I couldn't look at her any more. I needed a detail to claim my attention and began thinking of who would clean up the mess.

There were more shots in the dark and the sound of Will's breath getting louder. I crawled under my bed, curled up and stared at the decal of Dumbo the elephant on my yellow toy chest. I heard footsteps coming near in the dark. The door was pushed open. I could hear his breathing. It was so loud I couldn't hear my own. A shot sounded. He made grunting sounds like an animal in pain. Then there was quiet.

I didn't know how long I was there under the bed staring at the decal and pushing away the smell of death. I had no thoughts. I just stayed under the bed. After a while I wondered how I could be found. Mom was in front of the door and it didn't look like she was getting up. "It sounded like firecrackers," I told my grandfather when he found me under the bed.

I don't remember leaving the house. I was taken to my grandparents' house, bathed and settled into clean sheets. I could hear grownups talking and the phone ringing all night. I remembered the screech owl I had heard the night before outside our house. Now I knew why it had come and wished that I had told Mom about it then. I wished I had done a lot of things. But most of all I wished that Mom and Will had not left me behind.

I remembered other nights when I was very small and how creatures visited me when I was alone. Even though I was a baby then, when Mom and I were visiting relatives in Oklahoma, I remembered the nights clearly. The glow in the room from the hall night-light was the moonlight for me. I could feel it, golden and warm, through the opening of the door left ajar. Lying in a crib, I was waiting . . . waiting for the night animals. I could smell the soap that my mom used to scrub the floors, and I could hear the solid ticking of the grandfather clock that lived in my room because Mom could not stand its sound. I wasn't afraid. I was prepared, awake and calm in the soft light.

There were brown flowers with red centers in the linoleum. The contours of the uneven floor made a rolling landscape that had to be crossed for someone to get anywhere in the room. I knew it by heart—

each little nick, dent and faded spot, along with the smell of fabricated cleanliness. I also knew that the night animals had to cross this landscape to get to me and did not know it as well as I. Some were friendly, like the porcupine, and reminded me of *Unci*'s quill work. Others came as a challenge, like the wolves of my father, flashing their teeth. Every night they came.

There was no language for my knowing of these things as I lay in my crib waiting, listening to the ticks of the grandfather clock. Even when the mouse ran under the crib, I did not cry for my mother to console me. I waited and stared at the night-light because if I was still the owls would fly in and wrap their wings around me like my grandmother's arms. So in August in Iowa in my sixth summer with my cheek against an ironed pillowcase and the night filled with voices speaking of death, I curled up into the comfort of the spirit of Grandmother Mabel and *hinhan tanka*.

Two days after my mother's death, it was still August even though lifetimes had passed since my grandfather found me under the bed. I was sitting on the back steps of my grandparents' house. The air looked wavy from the heat and humidity. The house was filled with women cooking and talking in hushed voices. I could smell fried chicken, beans and cornbread. The voices hummed and sang and whispered secrets. Miss Jackson sang and prayed while she cooked. It was a low sweet gospel praying, accompanying the smell of good "soul food."

I was picking at the red paint on the porch, which had formed little bubbles from the heat. This was the day of my mother's funeral. My grandparents did not think it was good for me to go. They had an argument with Doc Wesley's wife. She thought it was wrong to keep me at home. She knew I had seen the screech owl. She told me she had heard one that night. She knew about owls and their messages, and she knew about good-byes. But my grandparents didn't know about good-byes for children. They were drowning in the torrent of their own grief and guilt. So I sat on the porch during the funeral, picking at the paint.

I was in a vacuum of nothing but me, the paint bubbles and the heat. Everything else had been sucked out by the sudden disappearance of my mother and the violence of her leaving. When my grandmother came back from the funeral, she came out onto the porch and sat down beside me. "Your mommy's gone to heaven," she said. I looked out at the lawn. The hollyhocks and honeysuckle were blurred against the house. Heaven seemed very far away in the heat-soaked Iowa sky. Miss Jackson's voice singing "O Precious Lord" came from the house like a breeze. I said, "No, she didn't go to heaven. She's on another radio station and I can tune her in whenever I want." From that moment on my grandparents were never sure about me.

Everything moved slowly into a routine after that, but death changed the look, the smell and the sound of my life. In one night I moved from a world that included the cabin at Pine Ridge to one that was at the center of the Negro community in Iowa. Crime always gets a lot of attention, and I was the present object of that interest. At first I was surrounded by the care and concern of the "mothers/sisters" of the neighborhood—women in white dresses with handkerchiefs splayed out in their breast pockets like floral arrangements. They pressed me to their bosoms, which smelled of hair grease and perfume; they brought pies and fried chicken to console me and my grandparents.

On Friday nights they gathered in the kitchen and cooked up a storm while their husbands and my grandfather picked up mandolin, guitar, mouth harp, spoons and any pots and pans they could get. The blues rang out the windows and down the street. My grandmother couldn't carry a tune but Miss Jackson and Mrs. Wilson would come out of the kitchen when the music got good and pretty soon they would start to sing. The words weren't important. They sometimes made fun of someone there or sang about a person who was sick or in love. But the sure thing was that they played and sang every Friday night, and they never sang about my mother.

After the funeral no one mentioned Grandmother Mabel or Dad, and when I asked about them or wanted to know when I could go back to South Dakota, I was greeted with silence or a change of subject. If they did answer, they reminded me that my grandmother couldn't read so there was no sense in sending a letter. Before I could say that I knew Uncle Billy would read it to her, they would move away from me into other conversations. I wondered if Dad and Billy knew that I was alone here and didn't care. I wrote letters to Dad and gave them to my grandparents to mail, but months later I found them in a box in the kitchen. After a while I was afraid to ask. I looked at the mail in the box every day for a sign from Pine Ridge, but nothing came. So I settled into the silence and my new life.

While I was learning the smells of smothered porkchops, sausage and gravy I was also learning my way around the neighborhood. I began to carve out my place with the other girls on the block by learning dance steps quickly, beating them out in double Dutch and joining the drum-and-bugle corps. I would dance by myself in the driveway with music pouring out from every house around me. Remembering powwow dances, I made up steps of my own and taught them to Tanya and Joleen across the street. I also had to fight, as the continuous taunts got to me. One day when I came home crying because Tony Mason had hit me, my grandfather took me back to the park and made me confront her. I either had to beat her then and there or face my grandfather and the endless comments from the kids about my mother. Tony was one of the tough girls, but I beat her and we became friends after that. Dancing and fighting secured for me a place in the neighborhood, but the whispering never stopped.

After a while my grandparents' friends started gathering in the kitchen after I had gone to bed, to talk about what they should "do with" me. I could get upstairs two ways: the front stairs, which everyone always took, and the back, "servants'" stairs, which led to the kitchen.

On the nights when they came to discuss my fate, I would sit on the back stairs just out of sight. They would keep their voices low, speaking about "the tragedy." I would listen till they stopped talking; then I would creep back up to my room and pretend to be asleep. I wondered if I would go to an orphanage and if *Unci* could find me there. I knew I wouldn't be going to Pine Ridge anymore.

School started in September, and the kids there whispered about me as had the grownups in the kitchen of my grandparents' house. Everything at school seemed to be made of concrete, and I missed the dirt of *Unci*'s. So I spent my time looking for a healing place—a shelter like those used by wounded animals who escape the killing.

Grandmother Gladys kept a perfect house, scrubbed and cleaned, so there were no dark corners in which to hide. I crawled into her closet with the smell of perfume and cedar chips. But the shoes neatly placed in rows on the waxed and polished floor did not offer comfort. I went secretly into the attic when everyone else was downstairs and looked for consolation behind the trunks and stacks of magazines. But eventually dampness and the promise of earth took me to the basement. Here the clothes were washed in the wringer machine, with a crank I loved to turn. I was always mesmerized by the sight of clothes coming flattened through the wringer, by the rising steam and the smell of soap and wet cement. It was also the room where we plucked and cleaned the chickens for Sunday dinner, so there was always the faintest smell of feathers seared in boiling water.

For days after school I investigated every corner in the basement. I began in my grandfather's workshop. I crawled underneath the work table where he had stashed things in one huge mound of work clothes, rags, tools and half-empty Lucky Strike packs. Everything else in the room had been stored in an orderly fashion by my grandmother—jars of nails in order of size, hooks for the tools, and shelves for those items that should be neatly put away in clear view. But there wasn't much room in the mound under Grandpa's work table, and the concrete floor did not welcome me.

I tried the storeroom with its shelves of canned goods. As tidy and well kept as the rest of the house, it did not offer healing and solace and a place to hide. I had almost given up when I went out the back entrance under the porch and noticed a big pile of lumber stacked in a dark corner. I crawled under the lumber and found what I had been looking for—a hole in the foundation wall. I couldn't see what was behind the opening, but I didn't hesitate. I crawled through the opening headfirst with my hands groping in the dark. I could smell damp earth as I touched the ground and pulled myself through the hole. I landed in a room-like space where I could stretch out and even stand up. I felt around in the dark, finding dirt floor, small pieces of wood and some very small bones. I had finally found my way home.

Every day after school I changed my clothes, had the snack my grandmother had made for me and asked to be excused to go and play. I would head out the front door as if I meant to cross the street; then I would walk around the side of the house quietly and go under the porch, into my refuge. I spent a year underneath the house trying to remember, to grieve and to heal.

Secrecy, the basement, and the earth made the ritual of my healing sacred to me. I gathered my ceremonial objects with care. I hid birthday candles I found in the kitchen and gathered matches, a difficult task for a seven-year-old, even in a house of smokers. I also collected and traded for the pennyknives which came in the gumball machines. In my cave, I burned away their blue plastic handles, watching the colors of the flames in the dark. I found red cloth in the sewing room so that I could make a bundle of the small bones I had found. I remembered the red cloth in *Unci*'s metal suitcase and the red tobacco ties on her nightstand. I made ties, too, but with dirt instead of tobacco.

This ritual was the thread that kept me connected to *Unci*, her ways and her language. I crawled through the hole and touched the earth with my hands, saying *Hau mitakuye oyasin*, words I had learned from her. I knew it meant "all my relations," and I wanted to be connected to my relations. I made my way to the red bundle, emptied my pockets of candles, and lit the knives, holding them until the metal got too hot. Then I laid them on the ground. I replaced the candles when they burned down. But sometimes I just sat in the dark and sang to myself.

This place kept me safe from the images too terrifying to remember and healed me from wounds I had forgotten. But slowly the memories came back with images, words and thoughts so foreign that I felt I was reporting on a horrible event in someone else's life. But in the remembering came the rest of the healing.

In that dark I found safety enough to remember my stepfather and why I was afraid of him. I remembered that after school on the days when Will came home early I would try to find a friend to bring home with me. Most times I took as much time as I could to get home, trying to make sure Mom was there. But when she wasn't, he told me I had to clean up after school. He took me to the bathroom and made me take off all my clothes while he washed his hands. He owned a print shop, and his hands had black ink caked under the fingernails. He was always trying to wash it off. He had a fingernail brush he rubbed on a bar of Lifebuoy soap and then used to scrub his nails. I hoped it would take a long time. I took off my clothes slowly. The bathroom felt crowded with him in it. He was so big there didn't seem to be room for me.

When he was through washing his hands, the room was filled with the smell of that soap. He sat on the toilet stool with the lid down and pulled me to him. He called it "checking me" to see if I needed a bath. He started rubbing my body, my chest and back. Then his hand went between my legs. He spread open my legs and unzipped his pants. I focused all my attention on the room. I knew every place where the blue paint was peeling from the steam. I made landscapes in my mind in the mounds of paint chips and dust which had accumulated under the radiator next to the bathtub. I counted the insects trapped inside the light fixture on the ceiling. I tried to leave my body. The ivory ceiling became moonlight, and I was back in Pine Ridge. I sat with *Unci*, and we said prayers for the little girl trapped in the bathroom. But most of all I didn't make a sound. I did nothing to make him angry.

When he finished he told me to get dressed and to remember that this was "our little secret." I never did tell Mom, but I knew she knew. When he wasn't at home we sat together on the couch hugging. We didn't talk much. Sometimes she told me stories about my dad and how soft his voice was. When I sat in the dark and remembered, I cried. I knew she must have been afraid of Will, too.

chapter four

Pehin */h a i r*

*Many times as a child I dreamt of Grandmother Mabel's hair and wished
for such silkiness in my own. So many of my childhood thoughts were
focused on my hair and on this wish. Years later, in the sword-sharp cold
of Wounded Knee, my memories of childhood pain concerning my hair
bumped up against others' bitter memories of the Negro Buffalo soldiers
fighting against the Lakota in the land of my ancestors. The wild African
presence in my hair connects me to those soldiers even in the eyes of some
of my relatives. In the midst of my homecoming and the Spirit Releasing
Ceremony for the Massacre at Wounded Knee, it was once again my hair
bringing looks and words that scraped these old wounds raw.*

In the days after my mother's death, Grandfather Burton and I were
so close I thought the bond would never bend or break. We were
inseparable. We went fishing, worked in the garden, made things and
read aloud to each other. I endured Catholic school and piano lessons
for him. He read me stories every night before bed, and the strength
of his voice was like the straightness of his back, something to lean
on, to give courage. Every day when he closed the barbershop and
came home, I was waiting at the side door for his car to come into

the driveway. When the door opened and he walked in with his Stetson cocked to one side and his pants riding low on his hips, I'd rush into his arms as he hollered, "Whoa, gal." My grandmother had his nightly shot of bourbon ready at the top of the stairs. It was the best part of my day.

In the neighborhood I was finding my place. Like other black kids in the late fifties, I watched the *Hit Parade* on TV while learning the hand jive; I sang a capella with the kids on the block and got my hair pressed every other Saturday. I danced at home, in the street and with my friends, and I had my first admirer. Although I knew that what I heard on the radio's top ten was white people's music, the music that seeped through every crevice of our neighborhood—from clubs and radios, from groups of kids singing in basements, and from after-hours joints on the weekends—was ours, rhythm and blues. I remembered Grandmother Mabel in my heart, but I was living as a black now. Even the word had changed from "Negro" to "black," as if the distinction were being refined.

Sometimes after I was tucked into bed, I crept down the back stairs to listen to the late-night conversation of my grandparents, just as I used to listen to their visitors. They were getting complaints from the nuns at St. Joseph's. I had been at the school three years, but I still did not feel as if I belonged there. Usually Burton would tell my grandmother to relax. One night in August I was sitting on the stairs biting my fingernails and listening half to them and half to the kids still playing under the streetlight. My grandmother was starting her pitch again. "I got another call from the sister. This time it was the principal. She says that Kaylynn just isn't adjusting to school or her classmates. Her grades are going down and she seems preoccupied. She thinks that we might even need to get her some help." I waited for my grandfather's standard response: "Just give the gal some time. She'll come around. Daisy was shy. Maybe she's just shy."

This time the end of the conversation took a different turn. My grandmother kept on. "Daisy was at least smart. Kaylynn's grades are getting lower and lower. I talked to that boarding school in Illinois, and they have room for her this fall. I think we should tell them she'll be coming." I felt like I had missed a vital chapter in the book. This was something I had never heard before. I crept down a few more steps and forgot about the kids in the street. I stared at the grain of the wood in the stairs as she went on, "You don't know how much trouble it has been. You're at the shop all day. It's just too much, Burton. At least at the boarding school we won't be worrying all the time."

"Okay, Gladys, go ahead. Have it your way, but I still think three hundred miles is a long way away." I felt as if the wind had been knocked out of me. I doubled up on the stairs and tried not to yell out. His words kept stabbing at me until the wound of his betrayal filled my whole body. The wood under my feet became cold and unfriendly, and the yellow paint on the stairwell rippled. I crawled back up the stairs and went to my room. I was covered in sweat, not from the August heat, but from the pain in my heart. I took the sheets from my bed and made a white nest next to the yellow toy chest that had saved me once. I wanted to crawl under the house back to the smell of dirt and to the bundle of small bones, but it was too far away.

I avoided them as much as possible the next day, until dinner, when they announced their decision. Gladys had wasted no time in confirming my place. I couldn't eat, but I didn't flinch. Grandmother Mabel had told me to save my tears, saying that they were powerful and not to be wasted. I sat watching Gladys and Burton eat as if nothing had changed. After dinner I went to my room and laid out all my gifts from Grandmother Mabel: the birch bark canoes and the birch bark box covered with quill work and filled with secret treasures. I wrapped them all in red cloth and took them down to my hideaway under the house. As I crawled through the hole and placed them on the ground where they would be safe, I remembered the pouch with my birth cord. It had disappeared in the haze after Mother's death. I hoped that wherever it was it would continue to protect me and connect me to *Unci*.

As the entire house filled with the activity of my leaving, I stood in the eye of the storm, silent. I helped sew name tags into all the new clothes Gladys had bought for me. I wondered why it was their name and not mine that was on my clothes. I would leave without my name and without the sacred gifts of Grandmother Mabel. Everyone spoke about my leaving as if it were an adventure, a vacation. No one asked how I felt or what I thought. No one talked about separation. We simply prepared for my departure as if there were no pain involved.

We drove most of the way in silence, not playing the usual games of reading Burma Shave signs and counting birds. We stopped in Centerville to visit the Fergusons, friends of my grandparents. Burton had planned the trip so we could spend the night there and arrive at the school during the day, since there might not be a motel for blacks in that town. And the Fergusons had a daughter, Bonnie, a few years older than I. We usually had fun together when we shared the bed in her room. This time it was so hot that we were allowed to sleep on the porch and stay up a little later.

Bonnie had never heard of boarding school. She thought it was a reform school and wanted to know what I had done wrong. We made a tent of sheets underneath the light on the porch, and I told her what I had heard of boarding school from Grandmother Mabel, who had often told stories about my dad going off. "They take your name away, " I said. "We sewed all these little tags on my clothes, underwear and everything, and it was my grandparents' name . . . not mine." The crickets emphasized my statement while I tried to remember other things I had heard. "You could run away," Bonnie suggested. But we discarded many plans, finally deciding that South Dakota was just too far away for a ten-year-old to go by herself.

The next morning, after only a couple of hours of driving, we rode through the center of the small Illinois town. We found the school at the other end of the main street. We were directed to a red brick building which stood alone on the west side of the street. It was the grade school residence. We were greeted at the back door by one of the nuns. She was Benedictine, different from the nuns at St. Joseph. Her habit had a stiff pleated white coif that bobbed when she walked. Her name was Sister Mary Francis, and she led us to the dormitory and locker room. Our steps echoed on the hardwood floor, and everyone we passed nodded politely but spoke in whispers as if we were in church. The walls were painted faint yellow like the blouses of the brown-and-yellow uniforms we were given. In the halls there were one or two paintings of St. Benedict and the Blessed Virgin.

My grandfather carried my bags to the dormitory. All twenty-eight girls in the grade school slept here, grouped by age and grade from the first through the eighth. Not many of them had arrived yet; the few other girls in the sixth grade were sitting on their beds staring at me. One of the nuns suggested that my grandfather take my bags to the locker room so that I might unpack. Then she took my grandparents aside and pointed out that they should leave before dark since there were no accommodations for "coloreds" in the town. I wondered why I was staying. I didn't go down to the car with them to say good-bye. The other girls were still staring at me, so I went to the locker room. Everything in that room was dark wood, like the stairs in Burton and Gladys's house. There was wood paneling on the walls, a lighter wood floor and dark wooden lockers. It smelled of clean laundry and cedar. I found my locker, crawled inside, curled up in the smell of wood and cried.

On the third day of school we were told to form a line. We were being led from the upstairs dormitory down the stairs and out of the building to the main dining hall. We were not to speak. That was an impossibility. It was our first excursion out of the building since we had all arrived, and the entire line was buzzing. When we entered the dining hall, the nun called for silence, but there was still a low hum and her gaze focused on me.

I tried to make myself invisible as she came down the line toward me. I could smell the food in the dining hall and the hint of disinfectant on the tile floor and walls. It was dimly lit in the hallway, and I thought she might be looking at someone else. She stood in front of me and leaned very close to my face, asking, "Did you hear me say, 'Silence'?" Her mouth was very dry, and the words clicked as she spoke them.

"Yes."

"Then why were you talking?" The white pleated coif was bouncing as she leaned closer to me.

"I was answering a question."

She took a breath, raised a leather glove which she had taken from her belt, and slapped me across the face with it, hissing, "Silence means silence." Her face was still close to mine and I did not hesitate. I slapped her back, knocking the perfect white coif and headpiece back so that a wisp of hair appeared.

The girls held their breath. All the air seemed sucked out of the hallway, leaving her and me in a vacuum of pink tile, shock and anger. We stayed like that, facing each other, as she recovered. I was mesmerized by the fact that she had hair. The vacuum cracked as she ordered the line to proceed to the dining room. She grabbed me by the arm and squeezed the words out between her teeth. "You stay here, you little heathen." I realized I was in for serious consequences.

She held me there until two other nuns arrived. I don't know how they heard. Perhaps it was like a signal sent through a beehive. She never let go of me. They marched on either side of her like sentinels as she escorted me to the chapel and pushed me toward the brass railing in front of the altar. The marble floor rang with our footsteps. I was forced into a kneeling position on the marble facing the altar. At first I rested my hands on the brass railing for balance, but the nuns quickly removed them, forcing me to balance all my weight on my knees. By then the priest had arrived.

The nun who had slapped me left, and the priest took me to the back of the chapel near the confessional while the other two nuns waited in the shadows. His name was Father Edwards, and he spoke in a soft soothing voice, but the words he said confused me. He told me nuns were the wives of Christ and were holy. He said that to strike a nun was a sacrilege, a desecration of the holy. I couldn't understand why Christ had so many wives, but I didn't question it. I simply wanted him to understand that she had hit me unjustly. I tried to explain it to him. But he held his hand up and shhhh'd me, wiping away my truth with his gesture. "You must confess your sin even before you apologize. Such a sacrilegious act is a mortal sin of which you must be cleansed."

"How can it be a sin when she hit me first?"

He sighed in exasperation. "Will you confess, daughter?"

"I don't see why I have to confess when she hit me first."

He motioned for the two nuns to come forward. He shook his head and left the chapel as the nuns led me back to the brass railing, pushed me down on my knees and lifted my arms into the position of Christ's outstretched arms on the cross. I was to remain there for the rest of the night.

There was always one nun in the shadows during the night. I remained there with the faint smell of frankincense and the sound of nuns singing psalms at the appointed hours. When my arms drooped, footsteps would click across the marble and I would be pulled back into position. They told me to pray if I knew how. I prayed to Grandmother Mabel to help me save my tears from the pain in my knees and arms. I looked at the Christ on the cross in front of me and felt some kinship. I wondered if he had saved his own tears for their power.

I surrendered the next morning and went to confession. I recited the prayers given as my penance and said my apologies with my mouth, but not with my heart. I went back to the dormitory branded a "heathen." Yet I was filled with the mystical connection I had made with the suffering Christ; I felt it shining in my heart and in my eyes. I found friends who thought I was brave and enemies who thought I was evil. Our teacher proclaimed me "proud as Lucifer" for my refusal to apologize immediately. I had found the place I would occupy till I finished school.

"Are you a nigger?" "Do Indians still take scalps?" "Can you get sunburnt?" "Does your hair hurt? Can I feel it?"

The days that followed were filled with questions asked by farm girls who had never seen brown skin and nappy hair. They focused all of their attention on my hair, like ravens descending on a carcass. I longed for any hair but my own. What I saw in the mirror was hair made of iron—curved and twisted like snakeback roads and wild as kudzu, a weed that grows like an unchecked brush fire. There were hundreds of questions, but those concerning my hair always came first, preceding me like a storm. The questions ambushed me from every corner until I learned to shield myself from these slings and arrows with silence or fists.

Every Friday was hair-washing day. It was a nightmare that haunted me throughout the rest of the week. The school rules said that everyone had to wash her hair on Friday after school. The bathroom was black-and-white tile with six toilet stalls and six sinks lined against the opposite wall. Girls were always sitting in the stalls waiting to use the sinks next; the room was filled with laughter, suds and the smell of shampoo. I would try to delay as long as possible. Water unleashed all the revolt and strident impudence of my hair. I would come away from the sink with a wild and unmanageable mass that required oil and strength to tame. There was no place in the bathroom or dormitory where I could wrestle it back into submission away from the questions and laughter of twenty-seven other girls.

I tried leaving class the moment the bell rang last period and running down to the bathroom where I had stashed my towel and shampoo so that I could be there before anyone else. I would pretend to wash my hair, cover it with a towel and then rebraid it in secret. One day a girl hid in one of the toilet stalls during the last period to spy on me and told the nuns I had not washed my hair. The next Friday Sister

Clare marched me into the bathroom after school. All the other girls crowded in the stalls and around the sink while she stood over me and watched me wash my hair.

I found escape in dancing. Every night after school I would change out of my uniform and into my own clothes, go down to the recreation room and dance. It didn't even matter if there was good music or not; just the movement of my body to my own rhythms brought me peace. There were a few girls from Chicago who frequently joined me, but I didn't mind dancing alone. If I got downstairs first I would pick the music, then teach steps to anyone who wanted to learn. There was one girl in my class, Carrie, who came pretty often.

First she just watched while I danced. I could see she wanted to join in but didn't ask. After a few weeks I forgot she was there, and then one day she just got up and started dancing with me. I was amazed at how well she had learned the steps sitting there watching. We became friends through the music, and then we discovered we had a lot of the same questions, such as why couldn't we read all the books in the library, and why couldn't we ask questions about other religions? We began to spend time together when we weren't dancing. We started dressing alike and exchanging clothes. We even created outfits for our new dance steps and named them before we taught them to other girls so our stamp would be on them. I had my first friend.

Carrie became my ally in the battle of the hair. She and I together had come up with the fake hair-washing idea, and she even helped me find places where I could oil and braid my hair in secret. We went to the grape arbor and hid among the vines so we could be in the sunshine. One Friday we even got under the covered grand piano in the auditorium. We were always looking for new places. Carrie lived in a small town not far from school, and her mom was a hairdresser. One Sunday when her mom was visiting, we asked her for help. She told us about electric combs and promised to bring one the next time she came.

When she brought the electric comb we hid it in the laundry basket in the locker room, because our lockers were inspected frequently by the nuns. When Friday came I washed my hair with everyone else and tied it up with the scarf. After the lights went out that night we waited until all sounds of squirming girls fighting sleep had subsided. We had devised a signal: Carrie would cough four times. After the cough we crawled out of bed and headed for the curtained cubicle of the dorm watch nun, Sister Clare. We met there and lay outside the white curtain until we were sure we could hear the deep breathing of sleep. Then we tiptoed our way out into the hallway and over to the locker room.

We crouched next to the window in the locker room. We had chosen this place because it was not connected to any living space and because it had an electrical outlet by the window; the moon gave enough light so that Carrie could see not to burn me. Facing the door to the hallway in case anyone came, we plugged in the electric comb and waited for it to heat up, giggling under our breath from fear and excitement. We had planned it well.

It was the first time since coming to school that I was not shamed by the unveiling of my hair in its natural state; Carrie never seemed disturbed by the sight. I combed out the tangles while she kept testing the comb to see if it was heating up. Then she worked her way through the mass, slowly, because this was foreign territory for us both. We stopped still when the oil I had used on my hair sizzled with the heat of the comb. We were sure the sound was as loud as it seemed to us.

Trust came back into my heart during that moonlight session and those that followed. It came with the respect I had for the risk she was taking. One whole semester we managed to sustain this ritual. But then we got careless one night and put the comb back in the laundry basket before it had fully cooled. The comb smoldered in the basket all the next day until one of the nuns found it. It didn't take long for them to guess who was involved. Getting caught and suffering punishment together only strengthened the bond of friendship. The nuns put us both in solitary, which meant that we were separated from all the other girls in class and in the cafeteria as well as in the dormitory. We spent all of our time alone together for two weeks. When it was over we were inseparable. We were best friends until Carrie left in the ninth grade.

Every summer my grandparents and I would travel. When I was first in boarding school, we spent summers in Mexico; later we went to Europe on package tours. We always traveled to places where being black was not a disadvantage. During these trips, which they thought absolved them from any guilt about leaving me at boarding school, I talked about my hair and begged them to find a way for me to fit in. (It wasn't until I was a junior that we discovered chemical hair straighteners.) After the comb incident, I spent the summer at the house they had rented near Mexico City nagging about a solution for my hair.

In the middle of seventh grade, after a conference between the nuns and my grandparents, it was decided that I could be exempted from the Friday shampoo rule. Instead I was to be taken once a month to a black beautician forty-five miles away to have my hair "done." So on a Saturday morning, while all the other girls were sleeping late or were in their pajamas eating donuts, I was collected by two nuns for my hair trip.

I had thought this might be a chance to see some countryside and forget about school. But the silent drive made me feel like a prisoner in a police car with the two nuns in front as officers, and I was unable to focus my eyes on anything in the passing landscape. We pulled up in front of a pink house with white trim; it was split-level and had an entrance for the beauty parlor near the garage door. There was a fenced-in yard with flowers growing everywhere, and I could see snake plants in the window. It reminded me of Dorelva's beauty parlor back in Iowa and Saturdays there with other girls. We parked at the curb rather than in the driveway. As we got out and walked through the gate, a woman came out to greet us. I had seen her looking out the window as we drove up.

Her name was Vera. She had on a pink pants suit pulled tight across a bust pointing straight out like a shelf. She smiled at me and gave me a hug as she led us to the side entrance. The nuns nodded a greeting without actually speaking and followed behind. The beauty parlor was in the basement. The room had fake wood paneling covered with magazine pictures of hairdos Scotch-taped to the wall. There were copies of *Jet* and *Ebony* on a small table next to a sagging couch with flowered upholstery. She motioned the nuns to the couch, saying, "Make yourself comfortable. We're gonna be awhile." She smiled at me again. Her smile took up the whole room and warmed it.

The room smelled like Royal Crown, the hair oil that came in cardboard and metal cans, and I could see the small gas fire and smell it, too. These smells, like the smell of the first rocks going into the sweatlodge, were such a comfort to me that I relaxed immediately. They were the smells of nourishment and shared secrets and represented a ritual space, a place of initiation. Across from the couch was a mirrored wall with a gas jet and a table laid out with hot combs and curling irons. Around the corner was a sink with a hose and a chair in front. Putting on a stained white smock, Vera took me to this shampoo chair. I got in and was squeezed into place by the weight of her bending over me. I was engulfed in the smell of her and the room. She shampooed my hair, wrapped a towel around it and then sat me down in front of the mirrors.

The nuns didn't move. They sat as if they had done this before; as if they had seen wild hair unleashed or hot irons pulled through tangled hair with the sound of sizzling grease. "Are you tenderheaded?" Vera asked. I shook my head and closed my eyes so I wouldn't see the black-and-white figures in front of me perched like Heckle and Jeckle. I fell into the safety of the smell, the sounds and the hands touching my head knowingly.

That Saturday and the ones after had their pleasure; I could feel my hair being treated with knowledge and kindness. I remembered that feeling each time I returned to school and was bombarded with questions about why my hair looked so different. The other girls never got used to the transformation even though it happened often. I would wait for the moment in the shampoo chair when Vera massaged my scalp. Even now when my head is stroked I close my eyes and drift on the pleasure of it. It is a rare thing.

In the years that followed I traveled on the unmarked trails that connect Indian Country in America. It is like traveling in a small town where memories bump up against each other, reshaping history in the contact. People came from all over the world to the one hundredth memorial of the Massacre of Wounded Knee. The horses from the Big Ride had ice forming on their nostrils at the graveside; the riders, their longcoats stiff from the cold, looked like warriors who had come back to the landscape. Even though I had found Lakota elders and teachers in Indian Country, I had not put my feet on this sacred land since I was six years old. My heart was filled with the discomfort of staying away from the land of my grandmother for so many years.

The grandmothers and aunties welcomed me back home, and there was much talk of my working at Pine Ridge, but in the center of the offer was the problem of my hair. Friends who had not left the reservation agreed that something had to be done about my hair. I had to look more like an Indian here. All of boarding school came back into view as I answered their offer. I found comfort in the memories of Vera and the women who now braid my hair. Though I knew no one would realize what they had triggered in me, I was reminded that my hair would not allow me to forget that I was never going to be all Indian. I thanked them for the offer and said I did not want colonized hair. We never mentioned it again. The solace and comfort I found on my return to my homeland came from the subzero skies of Paha Sapa, the Black Hills.

BECOMING

chapter five

Wokiksuye /

live and remember

The tension between the nuns and me continued, whether the subject was my hair, the way I always stayed outdoors or my constant questioning of instruction. They had taught me well how to use my intelligence, and my grandfather wanted me to be a straight-A student, so I read voraciously, anything I could get my hands on—especially books on philosophy and spiritual practices of other cultures. I found these books, for use by the nuns in their studies, stacked in the back of the library. The librarian, Sister Germaine, would leave them in a certain place for me, and I read them there and left them there. I didn't dare let anyone else find me with them, since comparative religion was a forbidden intellectual pursuit for the girls. We were discouraged from asking questions that went beyond the catechism, but I was looking for some connection to my own spirit in this world of thought. The pursuit of such connections between my own spirituality and the theology we were taught led me into direct conflict with the nuns.

The strain between the school and me was reaching the breaking point, and an episode occurred which led to my being expelled three months before graduation. My best friend, Camille, and I had decided to take our SAT tests together on a weekend at a nearby college. We had met Father Gerard when he came to substitute in one of our religion classes. He was to be in charge of us and we were very excited, since he had given us one of our first opportunities to express some of our philosophical ideas. He decided it would be a gift for us and his students to have an evening discussion of some of our ideas on comparative religion and spirituality.

We looked forward to our trip and even to the SAT test. When we arrived Father Gerard met us and took us to the student center, where we met and talked with other students well into the night. We didn't make it to the women's dormitory where we were supposed to sleep but stayed with one of the women who had an apartment off campus. The news of this reached our school before we did. And even though it was a priest who spoke for us, the worst was imagined.

In one day Camille and I were erased from the school as if we had never been there. Father Gerard lost his position at the university, and we lost our places as first and second in our class. We got up one morning and were called to see Sister Anthony, the principal. We waited in the hall on straight-backed chairs as she called each of us in separately and told us our parents were on their way to collect us. When we returned to our room under the guard of nuns, our things had been packed and our parents were there. It was over.

My grandparents were silent and enraged. They could not imagine a straight-A student being expelled; the two thoughts could not coexist in their minds. It never occurred to them that my story might differ from Sister Anthony's. So instead of asking me why it happened or how I felt, they devised a plan to get me back into school at home with an elaborate explanation as to why I was back so close to graduation. I can't remember the story they created, and it was clear that hardly anyone believed it; people in the neighborhood made up their own versions.

I dived into the world of public school and boys with the enthusiasm I had previously reserved for my studies. The school was close to

Burton's barbershop, so I rode to work with him, then walked the rest of the way. After being in school with a total population of 120, I was now in a teeming public school with 1500 students. There were no classes to match the level of study at boarding school, so I didn't have to devote much time to maintaining my grade average. I had been been studying French since sixth grade, and when I left I was taking fifth-level Latin and college-level English and math classes. The classes I needed for graduation in a midwestern high school were home economics and bookkeeping. So I was able to graduate second in my class. But academics was not nearly as engrossing as the sudden discovery of my sexuality. I had rarely been in a social setting with the opposite sex and found the stimulation overwhelming.

A boy named Bobby Gilliam had been busy that spring wooing all the light-skinned girls. It was obvious later that he had been doing more than talking pretty to us. He was attending West Point, and I was flattered by his attention. Boarding school had made me unfashionable and too naive for most of the boys from my neighborhood. So I was happy to be asked out. I didn't have many friends and wasn't privy to the gossip about him until I was part of it. Having had no guidance from my grandparents or family, I found myself pregnant by graduation. As a result of our one "date," I fell from being college bound to facing unwed motherhood.

It was a long fall, but I never considered marriage, even before I found out that one of my girlfriends in class, Toni, was pregnant, too. Everyone assumed I would have an abortion. My grandfather tried the hardest to convince me. He was sure that I would lose all sight of any future of college and a profession. I'm not sure if I said no just to go against him or because I felt Grandmother Mabel and her love of children near me. I was sure that having a baby would be really living, not just studying about life. When he figured out that I couldn't be budged, he gave me an apartment and agreed to pay the bills until the baby was born and I could get on my feet. Burton had invested long ago in apartment buildings in our neighborhood. He provided the low-cost housing for the community, and he furnished them for survival rather than beauty. I moved into one of them.

I graduated in 1963 and watched my belly grow through that fall, the time of Kennedy's assassination. By Christmas I was so large that not much was of interest to me. On Christmas Eve I looked around my apartment with boredom and a little disgust. The place was filled with furniture I had not chosen and floral wallpaper which made me nauseous. I tried to find something to watch on TV so I would not feel the loneliness and anger creeping in from the corners of the room. But it was Christmas, and there was nothing on for one who wanted to forget about family and home.

Dinner on Christmas day provided an opportunity for the usual age-old arguments and backbiting, with Aunt Georgia and Aunt Iris usually at center stage. Georgia's anger and desire to verbally wound anyone in her path always caught me off guard. None of us could figure out what had hurt her so badly and made her so bitter. I thought it might somehow subside with age, security or simply the joy of living, but it never did. Aunt Iris seemed to think that her Ph.D. made her an authority on any subject that came up and that other opinions were always lacking. Aunt Georgia talked to me as if I were an unwanted guest. Her tongue was as sharp as a razor, and the fact that she had developed cancer hadn't mellowed or tempered it. Some women at the beauty parlor said she stayed alive simply because she was too evil to die. Aunt Iris kept looking at me and shaking her head, talking about how I had thrown away my future. The rest of the family, cousins and aunts and uncles, filled the rooms, carrying constantly replenished plates of food. They sat in corners or around small tables making alliances. Everyone in our family saw himself or herself as the only one worthy of inheriting everything Burton had worked so hard to accumulate. I could see the family real estate and money being divided up as their eyes took inventory in the house.

I came back to the apartment stuffed with food and anger. My maternity clothes felt so tight that I put on the only thing that still fit, a red lace negligee Toni had given me when she found out we were both pregnant by the same man. She and I had become best friends. Her Italian mother was insisting that Bobby marry her to maintain the family honor. Toni was sure that her pregnancy was more valid than mine, even though the father was the same. I was glad my family was at least not pressuring me in the same way. I knew that marriage was not the solution. I looked at the nightgown and wondered about her and about the wedding that would happen in June after the baby was born.

I fell asleep on the couch and woke the next day still bored and uncomfortable. Hoping for a distraction, I reached for a novel I had been reading and tried to make myself comfortable, but I was all stomach. Aunt Vivian, who lived downstairs, said I was pointed because I didn't have a wide enough pelvis for the baby. All I knew was that my legs were starting to go numb because the baby had gotten so big it was pressing on a nerve. Lying down was my best position, even if it was hard to get up. I fell asleep to the sound of Christmas carols coming from another apartment. Suddenly I woke up with terrible cramps, my clothes wet. I knew the water had broken, and that it must be time to go to the hospital.

I was scared and rattled, and for once this room with its grandmotherly wallpaper looked comforting. It didn't occur to me to call anyone for help; all I could think of was getting to the hospital. I started wondering if I could fit behind the steering wheel. I guessed I could push the seat all the way back and put pillows behind me so I could reach the pedals and still have some give between me and the steering wheel. Slowly I began to change my clothes, sitting down when the pains came, a little in awe that I was coping with it. As I made my way to the garage, my clothes were already getting wet again with sweat. Thankfully the sidewalk and paths were clear of ice and snow by then.

By the time I got the garage door open and fit myself behind the wheel, I was completely drenched with sweat and chilled from the December air. The pain took all my attention and breath.

It was only a five-minute drive to the hospital, but the deserted streets stretched out in front of me like lonely desert roads going nowhere, and my labor pains made the blocks look like miles. I kept pulling over to the curb, hoping that some miracle would make them go away completely. But each time one subsided, another took its place. When I arrived at the emergency entrance I left the car there, keys and all. Nurses rushed towards me as I came through the doors, and in minutes I was in a gown between crisp white sheets with Aunt Vivian patting my hand and saying, "It's all right, baby. I'll stay with you." I had forgotten she was a nurse there, even though it was why I had chosen that hospital in the first place. She wasn't really related, but she had been "Aunt Vivian" to me all my life. She was my saving grace living in the apartment building. She visited often and kept my spirits up as she had done when I was a child and visited her every month while Burton was collecting rent from the other tenants.

The bed was curtained off, and I could hear the moans of a woman in the next bed. Everything seemed unreal; I drifted on images floating up around the white curtains between the women on either side of me. Everything was so crisp compared to how I felt. I sank into the valleys of relief between the pains, not knowing where I could find the strength for the next one. The doctor, coming in his white coat every half hour or so to see how I was doing, seemed irrelevant. The nurses who wiped me off and checked my dilation, and Aunt Vivian, who was always there, pulled me back from the pains with their jokes and their touch. The sounds of the women behind the curtains continued as I stifled my own moans. Sometimes there were screams. I wanted to scream, too, but I kept thinking, "I'm seventeen. I can't scream like that. They'll think I'm a baby." I didn't want to make any noise, and I still remembered to save my tears.

Once in a while when someone came through the curtains, I could see husbands through the openings, pacing and waiting. Then I felt alone and ashamed. These feelings lay at the corner of my mind even as the baby was being born. Sometime in the early evening the pains gave way to birth. As I pushed on command and held my screams inside my throat, Aunt Vivian held my hand and whispered, "Almost here." When the baby's head appeared, we both began to laugh. But even as I first saw my daughter lying in my arms, my shame stretched over us. I wanted to shield us from what people might think. We had only each other, this girlchild and I, and everything around us said this was not enough. I found comfort in her smooth black hair and tiny hands and feet, and nursing her held us together in a way no one's thoughts could violate.

I waited two days to name her and then picked a name which reminded me of better times. During the period when, as a child, I lived under the house healing myself, I had a recurring vision that I could not explain. I was in a palace with crystal chandeliers and an entire wall of gilt-edged mirrors. In the center was a table nearly a block long, covered with soft white lace and gold and silver trays of food. Each place setting had its own lamp and a small telephone. Around the outside of the table was a track where trays of food were moved around on a small train. I was at the head of the table. I was dressed in a white satin gown with a bustle and gold embroidery, and I was dancing. Everyone watched in silence and waited till I finished and sat down before they began to eat or called the train to deliver food.

It wasn't until I was twelve when my grandparents took me to France and we visited Versailles that I saw a room anything like what I had imagined as a younger child. This room, called the Hall of Mirrors, was a return to the familiar territory of my vision. After the vision I began dancing lessons (tap and ballet), even though I had danced in my own way for as long as I could remember. I put on performances for my grandparents whenever I came home for short vacations from boarding school. All my dreams of the future involved being an artist and living somewhere in Europe. So I named my daughter Denise in memory of France and the splendor I had seen there and to express my dream of being an artist. Then I began to learn what living was about.

I went back to Burton's apartment with my daughter and received lots of baby gifts from the family. I found a job and a baby-sitter and began the overwhelming life of a single mother at seventeen. I was glad I had learned to type, because I was able to get an office job at a decent wage the first day I went out looking. Toni was still my best friend, but her marriage to Bobby had changed things. She had settled into family life, and Bobby did not want us to spend much time together. I had few other friends, and the ones I did have were single and didn't want to spend their time with someone who had to take care of a child. Denise and I made our own world in that apartment. We spent a lot of time with Burton and Gladys, listening to family stories. I enjoyed my daughter and the laughter and wonder she brought to my life. I also longed for the dreams of an artist's life, which I had left behind. The work of raising her alone was so much more than I had ever imagined. By the time she was two I felt that I was dragging my life behind me like an enormous boulder on an uphill road.

Some days I would forget about the struggle of it as I watched her play outside and disappear into someone's yard, returning with a handful of flowers for me and falling down with laughter as she tried to eat the blossoms because they were so beautiful. But in the mornings when I had both of us to feed and get ready, and when I often had barely enough gas money for the trip to the baby-sitter and then to work, I felt very tired.

In June of Denise's second year, the summer heat was beginning, and I was wishing for a day with nothing to do as I pulled up in front of the Cundersons' just after work. Their house always looked inviting even though the brown paint had peeled away to almost nothing and the backyard was crammed with junk Mr. Cunderson had found while collecting garbage. They had adopted a boy Denise's age and had been baby-sitting her since both were newborns. The two of them were playing in the front yard, holding hands and kissing each other, then falling down backwards laughing. They still both walked with legs wide apart, as babies do at first to keep their balance. Mrs. Cunderson was sitting on the porch sewing and rocking back and forth on a swing.

"You sure look tired," she commented as she stopped her work to look at me over the top of her glasses. "You're too young to look so tired. Come up here and sit with me. These kids ain't in no hurry to stop playing and I ain't in the mood to start dinner yet."

I was so tired and she made the swing look so inviting that I sank into the pillows of it as if it were a bed. "There just doesn't seem to be any time for me," I began. "There's always washing or cleaning or cooking or shopping or work. Does it ever get any better?" My words extended in a long sigh as I settled into the swinging motion with her.

She smiled at me, shaking her head. "Sometimes it's easier when there are two of you, but there ain't no guarantee 'bout that. Ya know, family can help, too." I looked at her sideways, doing what my grandma called "cutting your eyes." I knew the price of family help, and I wasn't interested in any more of it. My family always "knew best" how to help me without ever asking me whether I needed or wanted it.

"You got other family, ya know," Mrs. Cunderson continued. "I never said nothing 'bout this before but your daddy and I got to know each other when he was here visiting you and your mama. I got some Indian family, too, so we used to talk." I couldn't quite focus on what she was saying. The words were going in but their meaning eluded me. "After he and your mama divorced we kept in touch for a few years. We wrote him when she got killed but the letter came back. Didn't know where he went. A few weeks ago we got a letter from him with a phone number and we called him up. He didn't even know Daisy was gone, just thought she didn't want no part of him. Your stepdaddy had made her return any money Art sent for you, so he had stopped sending it. He was real excited to hear about his grandbaby. He'd like to see y'all."

Memories were swarming around my head like flies around honey on a summer day. Thoughts I had put away for safekeeping brushed over me like wings. Grandmother Mabel's smell came to me, the scent of sweetgrass. Mrs.Cunderson was still talking. "He said his mother passed on so he moved away from South Dakota. Lives in Kansas now."

The whirring thoughts in my head stopped, frozen in place, when I heard *Unci* had died. Anger started in my toes and rose up through my body and out of my mouth as if he were the cause of her death. "If he waited all this time to find out about me, he can keep right on waiting. I want no part of it. There is no family there or they would have been here for me a long time ago." I wanted to push him away with my anger so that I could try to keep *Unci* alive. It never occurred to me that this might be the only chance I would get.

Mrs. Cunderson didn't try to convince me, and she never brought it up again. I never knew if she continued to write to him. At that moment I didn't want to see my father. I didn't want a connection to Pine Ridge if *Unci* was gone. I didn't want to be close to anyone again; it always seemed to end in pain. Getting up every morning and trying to find the energy and the money to care for Denise and myself was all the pain I could manage. My dreams of traveling to Europe again, of being an artist . . . they were all swallowed up by the amount of energy it took to survive.

Whenever there was a pause in my life, perhaps during Denise's afternoon nap on a weekend or when she was absorbed in her play, my dreams would creep into my peripheral vision and a kind of melancholy would settle over me. Not having the energy to resist, I simply waited for it to pass. On a day when I was in one of those ripples of melancholia, I picked up Denise at the regular time from the Cundersons and took her home, too tired for anything but feeding us and crawling into bed. As I was preparing dinner I could feel a shift, a stillness like the silent moment before a tornado hits town when the air appears to have turned a slight shade of green. I was wrapped in that silence while I cooked. Even Denise's voice came to me muffled, as through some kind of filter.

Later, lying in bed, I started to have pains, but I had no strength to get up and take something. So I let myself drift between dreaming and the pains. In the dream I was lying naked in a small stream, bleeding between my legs. Not only was blood flowing out but all of my organs as well. I didn't seem scared. I just sat watching as the entire stream became red with my blood. The part of me that wasn't dreaming was alarmed and kept shouting at me. I finally woke up.

The sheets were soaked with blood; I was burning up with fever. I tried to walk to the bathroom, but I had to drag myself. I couldn't think what to do. Through the window I could see the sky lightening to the soft gray that comes before dawn. I didn't know what time it was, but I reached for the phone to call the Cundersons. I didn't want to wake up Denise until I knew what was going on.

The Cundersons arrived before I could even get to Denise's clothes. Mrs. Cunderson took one look at me and phoned for an ambulance. She yelled at her husband, "Harry, you take that baby and go on home. I'm goin' to the hospital with this child here." I started giggling. It seemed so absurd to be going to the hospital. I had been fine yesterday, but now I couldn't even keep her face in focus as she placed towels between my legs to soak up the blood.

It was a week before the uterine infection was under control and I could get out of intensive care. Burton and Gladys were in Hawaii, so Mrs. Cunderson kept Denise. But by the time they got back from their trip, I was in my third week in the hospital, and social services had taken Denise and placed her in foster care. Neither social services nor my grandparents considered Mrs. Cunderson an adequate caregiver in my absence, even though she had cared for Denise every day before that. The arguments about this let me know that things had quickly gotten beyond my ability to understand and cope. My grandparents saw foster care as the beginning of the loss of my child to the welfare system and were shocked to have something like that happening in their family. Even as they were busy validating my unfitness as a mother, I was seeing any dreams I had managed to keep alive go up in flames, fired by mountains of guilt and hospital bills.

Burton got temporary custody of Denise; she was at home with them by the time I was released. They had given her my old room, and it was good to see her in a familiar place. It must have been terrifying for her in foster care, and I was glad we were reunited. Even so she was scared and disoriented and clung to me from the moment I walked through the door. It seemed good for her to be back with family no matter what they thought of me. She had always been close to Burton and called him PawPaw. They were playing together when I arrived, and, rested from my three weeks in the hospital, I joined in. The stay in the hospital had been my first rest since Denise's birth, so I was refreshed and glad to see her, but I was also dreading the never-ending cycle of work.

The second night I was home from the hospital, the family held a council: Burton, Gladys, Aunt Iris and Aunt Georgia. Even though I was sitting right there across from them at the dining room table, they talked about me as if I were invisible. I felt disconnected, too. Denise didn't know her future as well as mine was on the table, so we played in the delight of being reunited and of being fed and cared for by someone else. We went into the living room and she crawled into my lap, laughing, as we looked at her favorite picture book. Deep in the creases of our laughter I could hear Burton telling the others that I was smart enough to go farther if I had a chance. My dreams flew in from some distant place to flutter around those words, but I went back to playing, as Aunt Georgia and Aunt Iris left the house. The dreams still floated around me like a gossamer scarf.

When Aunt Martha and Uncle John arrived the next day from Cleveland, I was called into the dining room. John was related to

Burton but had been able to stay out of the family arguments simply because he was so quiet by nature. His wife, Martha, did all the talking. When they arrived my grandmother laid out the best china and silver for lunch, so I knew this was an important event. We sat down like strangers: Burton, Gladys, Aunt Martha, Uncle John and I. Denise was in the kitchen with Aunt Iris, who had come to baby-sit.

I was glad of Burton's abruptness, because everyone was sitting so still I was afraid to breathe. "We've had a talk, gal. Last night we called up John and Martha and asked them if they might want to take Denise so you could get on your feet. We all think it would be a real blessing for all of you. John and Martha can't have kids of their own and they have plenty of money for giving Denise a good home and education. I believe if you got the time and freedom to put yourself together you could be somebody. And we're all family, here to help each other. Denise would still have PawPaw and all her relatives. You think about it, gal. They're ready to take her home with them right now so you can start making a life for yourself."

I wasn't sure this was really happening. It felt like the delirium when I first got to the hospital. John and Martha kept looking at the floor. I knew everyone was waiting for me to say something, but I couldn't think of what it should be. I had no feelings about what was going on. It was too big for me to be able to take in. The silence went on a while. Then Martha started to talk. "She'd have two mothers. Even though you would sign adoption papers so we can do whatever we need to do for her, she will always know you are her mother and a part of our family."

I wasn't thinking of this as a choice; it was simply what was happening. So I said, "Yes." I kept sitting at the table after everyone left. When the room was empty and I could hear Burton and Gladys talking low in the kitchen, I went up to my room and lay on the bed, looking at the ceiling. There were no thoughts in my mind. It was as if I had been wiped clean. I slept for two days. John and Martha left right after lunch with Denise. They didn't take any of her clothes. I didn't see Denise again before they left, so I guess it had also been decided that good-byes would only be painful.

I woke up still numb. When I came downstairs Burton told me that he had paid the hospital bill, and he handed me a check. "You got two choices now. Me and your grandma are going to Africa for a month. You can come with us and get straight what you want to do or you can take this money and try to get yourself sorted out here." I didn't even look at the check at first. I had no idea what to do next. While they packed for their trip, I looked at a map of the United States trying to find some inspiration. They had given me enough money to find another apartment and take a couple of months to get settled. They didn't ask me any questions about what I intended to do since they were preparing for their trip. So with the freedom to choose anything, I bought a used car and headed for Chicago on the day they left for Africa.

During the trip I ran into some stormy weather, the kind that brings in tornadoes to rearrange midwestern towns. As I passed through each place in the landscape, it seemed as if the weather would let up and the green soupy clouded sky would make a way for me to get through. I thought about Denise and hoped that life was making a clear way for her, too. I missed her laughter and energy and found that in some moments I did not know what to do with myself in her absence. So much of me had been devoted to taking care of her.

I had chosen Chicago because I could get lost in the crowd and because Arthur, Aunt Georgia's son, said he could get me a job through the employment agency where he worked. I had phoned him when my finger landed on Chicago on the map. I was trying to find an apartment, and Arthur reminded me that Mom's brother, Junior, and his wife lived nearby, saying that maybe I could stay with them for a while. He gave me moral support while I made the call; they told me to come right over. Kathy wanted to know about Denise and why she wasn't with me. I tried to tell the story as coherently as I could, but I could see disapproval in her eyes. Junior didn't say anything. When her friends came over later, she introduced me by saying, "She's just given away her baby so you all treat her good. She'll be staying here while she recovers." Right then I decided I could find an apartment in a week. I found one in four days on the north side as far away from Kathy and Junior as I could get.

Arthur found me a job right away. I went to his office at the employment agency to fill out the application, and he introduced me to the person sitting at the next desk. I couldn't remember the man's name, but I remembered his eyes, which looked like blue ice. I kept thinking about them for the next couple of days as I settled into my new apartment and new job as a secretary at the local radio station.

In high school I had read a book in which the heroine, who is twelve years old, stands naked in front of the mirror and calls up the image of her dream lover. I had been so stricken with the idea that I had done the same. My dream lover had black hair, blue eyes and the soul of a poet. Denise's father had definitely not conformed to such an image, and I had temporarily lost sight of it. But in my first week in Chicago it came back to me when I saw Michael Sullivan sitting next to Arthur in that office.

Arthur invited me over to dinner to celebrate my first paycheck. I was glad for some kind of social activity and happy that I knew at least one friendly person in the city. I planned to bring along a bottle of wine and thought that Arthur and I would reminisce about our childhood and tell family horror stories. Arthur had lived with and laughed over the family's denial and disapproval about his being gay. No one said it out loud, but they always bowed their heads and pursed their lips when they talked about him. We had played together during summer vacations, and I had always known. Now we had a chance to be closer than ever in our semiexile from the family.

When I arrived at Arthur's apartment and rang the bell, I could hear him hollering for someone to answer the door. I thought there must be other guests. When the door opened I was greeted by those same blue eyes I had been remembering. Now they were clear and full and warm, and I could also see cheekbones and a mane of black hair. I didn't say anything at first, and Arthur came up behind. "You remember Michael, don't you? He's my roommate. We both got tired of living at home and found this place." I just kept looking at him. Arthur took the wine out of my hand and pulled me into the kitchen to help with dinner. I wondered if they were lovers but found an answer in the way Michael was looking back at me.

While Arthur and I cooked, Michael came in to pour some wine and keep us company. Talking, we soon forgot about both Arthur and the food. I found out that he had been in Germany in the army and wanted to return to Europe. I told him about my trips to Europe with my grandparents, about how much I wanted to go back. I even had the nerve to tell him my dream about Versailles. It was the first time I had spoken about that dream out loud, and he didn't laugh. He just said, "Maybe we can go there together." By the time we had finished the first course, Arthur had given up trying to join our conversation. A group of Arthur's friends arrived and saved us from feeling rude. After dinner we moved our conversation into his room.

It was dark; I felt as though I were crawling into a cave. When my eyes adjusted to the light, I could see pieces of silk draped over lamps and paisley fabric covering the bed. I felt like I was in another time and place. We lay on the bed and I fell into the blue of Michael's eyes. We were already starting to weave our dreams together.

In a week he moved in with me, and we delighted in decorating the place I had rented. We discovered our tastes were very similar. It was the sixties, and paisley throws from India covered our second-hand furniture; we both felt right at home. I was promoted to advertising. Michael had left the employment agency and begun working as a photographer's assistant. We were so busy creating a new life that we didn't notice any danger signs. We met each other's friends and spent a lot of time at the local bar with photographers and journalists; we didn't feel different from anyone else. Michael drank and lived with the passion of an Irishman, or at least what we both thought that was.

On New Year's Eve in 1968 we were married, and two months later we set off for Europe, grasping our dreams like luggage. We were heading for a life where, we thought, there would be no preconceived opinions of us. We had already begun to merge. One night while making love we stared in each other's eyes so long we couldn't remember who was who. We knew we were a racially mixed couple, but it was hard to remember who was white and who was brown. We were sure that was a good thing and nothing to be concerned about.

We left Chicago on a Greyhound bus for New York, our Icelandic air tickets to Brussels in hand and one suitcase between us. We had not planned for the trip financially and had only about two hundred dollars for buying basic camping gear when we arrived. When we landed in Brussels, we found a cheap bus to Paris and sat staring out the window holding hands in disbelief.

We arrived in Paris filled with romantic notions of finding work and living as exiles. We had left the States in the midst of the furor following the 1968 Democratic National Convention, and we got to Paris during the student protests there. It seemed that the whole world was molding a new future just like we were.

The illusions we had about life in Europe disappeared as we made our way south to warmer weather, having bought a sleeping bag and minimal gear. We began with the notion of hitchhiking, but, considering my schoolgirl French and Michael's shyness with strangers, we finally decided on walking. We knew it would take longer but didn't consider that we would run out of money. By the end of three months of walking and sleeping in the woods or by the road, we had developed a way of soliciting food from farmers or simply taking the day's ration from any hand that would offer it.

Being with Michael even in the hardest of times was like bringing dreams to life. Passion poured from him with every breath, and we sang and wove stories as we walked along the roads of France and Italy. We created all kinds of characters for ourselves so that we could negotiate difficult moments with each other at little cost. Often we pretended to be children or played games in which we mutually agreed upon our role as antagonist or protagonist. We had fantasy characters of princesses, monks, popes, kings, knights and maidens in distress. These allowed us to sidestep the messy emotional terrain we sometimes found ourselves in. I molded myself into the visions Michael had of us as "star-crossed lovers" leading a charmed and perfect life. We lived as if we were inhabiting a breathtaking novel. Michael had personas for each occasion and loved enriching the theater of everyday life with new scenarios. Hunger and bad weather only added to the drama and mystery.

This sustained us for a while, but by the time we got to Milan our money had dwindled to nothing, and we began to make more practical plans. We pawned the last of my jewelry in order to feed ourselves while looking for a ride to Munich. Following the suggestion of two GIs we met in Munich, we made our way to a small town in Germany on the Aurach River. Just at the edge of the autobahn, we found a truck going the entire distance. We had the first good sleep in several days and dried out our gear in the back of the truck.

When we arrived in Herzogenaurach, Michael found a job repairing slot machines for the army bases in the area. The man he worked for had married a woman from a nearby town and he had started the slot machine business when he left the service. After Michael had worked there a few months and I had learned my way around the community, I asked if there was a job for me. I had been learning German from the other women in our building, and I knew enough to answer a few questions at the interview. I was able to understand that each time the interviewer referred to me she called me "*die Schwarze*" ("the black"); still, this was a chance to get out of the house and improve my German.

We worked there until the boredom of ordinary life pushed us out of the country and back towards our dreams.

We lived on the edge of town in an apartment building mostly housing other foreigners who had come to Germany to work, although there were some retired German couples. The building was old, and living conditions were rudimentary. We didn't have running water in the apartment, and there was only cold water in the hall where all the toilets were.

Every Monday the women would get together with our laundry and begin early in the morning carrying water down to the basement to big washtubs which had fires built under them so we could boil and stir the clothes until we all agreed they were clean. Afterwards we would rinse them in tubs of cold water, hang them in the yard and have coffee and cake together. They brought magazines and would point to things and say words for me. They taught me the most practical and comical country German.

Frau Paul, with her dirndl and brightly rouged cheeks, was the most eccentric of the women in the building. She kept herself slightly distant from the others, but after the wash she would beckon me into her apartment to show me her collection of dolls and a kitchen filled with birdcages and birds. Her husband's Nazi war memorabilia covered every other wall. It was a strange and schizophrenic relationship we had on these Mondays; so distant from my home, it was the wash days and the quiet visits with the birds which connected me to Grandmother Mabel and my childhood. The smells of steaming wash and of the long-burning wood fire, followed by my hearing the names of the birds in another language, reminded me of those days of earliest learning.

Our apartment looked out over the Aurach River, and I spent many hours watching the ducks and looking at *Time* magazine just for something to read in English. During the days, the light shifted so that the shadows made presences in the room. I would watch a shepherd across the river leave every morning and return every evening with his sheep. Even with my job I had a lot of time to reflect. I would tentatively run my thoughts across the edges of my decision years ago to let Denise go. I never brought it into full view, so that I would not have to judge myself, but I would sample the thought of having her with me. Each year that we were apart, such an arrangement seemed more unlikely.

One afternoon Wolfgang, our only real friend, came by on his way back from a visit to his hometown. We drank coffee and watched the river, and in the middle of the conversation I realized that my whole way of perceiving the place changed when I spoke German. In the year since we had arrived I had become comfortable enough in the language so that I could feel the shift. I realized that even portions of my dreams were now in German. I couldn't translate some words into English. It was a feeling of accomplishment, yet at the same time it made me sad. I wasn't sure what this language meant to me. Knowing more German than Lakota made me feel very far from home, from my childhood and my past. I had never thought about Lakota as another language, since my memories of it were tied to experiences and made them whole. These memories were fragmented now; it had been years since I had heard the words in context. It was only in learning German that I realized I had words for some things that could not be translated into English and so could not be translated into German.

Michael changed jobs and started working at a nearby base. I quit my job and spent a lot of time with the women of the village. Our life was more secure, but we knew this was not why we had left home. We talked about our plans and dreams every night, and, after two years in Europe, we decided to visit our friends, Nettie and Brian, near London to see if we liked it and to get back to an English-speaking country. We had bought a car through the army and drove to High Wycombe, where Brian and Nettie lived. It was summer, so Nettie had time to show us around the countryside and take us into London.

Since it was clear to us after a few days that there were more opportunities here, we stayed. Nettie and Brian let us live with them in their cottage outside the city, and I tended the garden, baked bread and did most of the cooking for the household. It felt good to be working in the earth and caring for people for a while. Living in the cottage was inexpensive, so I got a part-time job at a local bookstore and spent most of my time working on the house and garden and making things. Michael found a job at a nearby factory. Nettie was an elementary school teacher, and Brian worked as a mechanic even though they both played in a rock band. They liked to try out new things and joined us in exploring England.

Our life was good and full, but we both felt that our dream still had not been revealed. That first winter, when we were all caught in the gray, damp boredom of English weather, Nettie got a leaflet about a dance center in London. She and I had both danced as children and thought it would be fun to take a class; to my surprise, Michael agreed to go with us. It was a good excuse for us to get into London. The center was near Covent Garden, and we parked there and stopped outside to build up the nerve to go in. A class was just finishing as we entered. A tall thin man about six feet four inches, in bright green bell-bottom dance tights and an orange tank top, was doing a combination of steps across the floor with a class of twenty or more following row by row. The wood floor was shiny with sweat and the mirrors were partially steamed. Someone opened a window. The man shouted, "Again." As Michael watched the students move across the floor with sweat flying off them and heard their breathing over the music, his stereotype of dancers was shaken. He was surprised at how difficult the steps looked and was anxious to join in and try them himself. He picked up the exercises right away and did really well, but when it came to the dance combinations across the floor he was at a loss. My dance training came back to me, and I enjoyed making the effort to keep up. We laughed at our mistakes but kept on trying.

By the end of that month we were both taking three classes a week in the evenings after work. It seemed as if the dream we had been pursuing over the past years had finally materialized. That first class had pulled us into dance with all our hearts. But we needed to move closer to London and find a way to dance every day. Nettie and one of her friends came with us for a while, but their passion was the band and it wasn't long before they stopped joining us. So Michael and I moved from High Wycombe to a shared flat near Portobello Road and the market there. Our flatmate was a costume designer who was hardly ever home, and our room was big enough for everything we owned plus a couple of pieces of furniture which we bought at the flea market. Now that we were in the city Michael began taking classes every day and started to get some of them for free as a demonstrator. We kept to ourselves and spent our time, energy and money on dance.

After six months of classes, Mike, the tall thin teacher of the first night, urged Michael to audition for the Rambert School of Ballet. I helped him fill out the application and watched him focus all his energy on classes before the audition. When the day finally came we sat in a coffeehouse down the street from the Rambert School for two hours watching the young girls go in for class. I waited there while Michael went in for the audition; as he walked toward the school carrying his dance bag, he looked very much like a dancer. When he passed the audition and was granted a full scholarship, dance filled every crevice of our lives. We celebrated with a party at Mike's, and Michael talked about his dream of choreographing. Even while he had been preparing for the audition, Michael had known he wanted to be a choreographer. He pushed his own body to find out what other bodies could do.

With Michael's scholarship, our lives changed. He was at Rambert all day and found a job ushering at Sadler's Wells Theatre at night so that he could watch as much dance as possible. I found a job as administrator of a small ballet company. I still took classes whenever I could and worked at the theater with Michael when I had time.

Michael finished his two years at Rambert in 1974 and began choreographing. I found it hard to believe that we had been in Europe for six years. It was only phoning home and receiving news of Denise and the family that made me realize I had been away so long. We began living the life both of us had dreamt. The small company I managed gave us a bedsit in their building. It was an enormous house, once owned by a friend of Aldous Huxley, which had been converted. Each member of the company had a room on one of the upper floors; the office was in the basement. The large ballroom was used as the main rehearsal space, and what had been a painter's studio was the artistic director's private studio. The whole company lived, worked, played and fought in that enormous house. Michael was allowed to use the studio and was finding that he liked choreographing as much if not more than dancing. Since the other dancers were older and already committed to dancing the work of Alexander, the company's artistic director, it seemed natural for Michael to choreograph for me as his partner, even though I didn't move with the same passion in the work. He had friends who had been at Rambert who worked with him some-times, but in the end we danced and worked together because it was convenient.

Even friends who didn't like all his work agreed Michael was gifted. Everyone spoke of his talent and his future. I didn't stop to ask myself if it was what I wanted. We were the charmed couple, exotic and daring. When we weren't dancing, we were at the theater, drinking in the magic, standing in the dark at Sadler's Wells transfixed by the work of Paul Taylor, Alvin Ailey, Louis Falco, Merce Cunningham and Hans Van Manen. We would stand in the last row, holding hands, trembling with excitement as we watched things we had never imagined possible. It was our education and initiation. London allowed us to be poor and eccentric and to go to the theater as often as we liked.

The house and the company became home and family. Our room was a sanctuary and the studio the place of visions. I had painted the floor in our room shiny black so that all visitors had to take off their shoes when they entered. I was continually waxing it to keep the black sheen, but I loved the feeling of stepping into another world. Every evening we threw the dance bags in, took off our shoes, found shillings for the space heater and fell onto the bed. I had painted the walls shades of earthen brown, so that we felt as if we were being embraced. We sat on the floor, drank tea and told our stories. We were sure this was the life for which we were suited.

Somewhere in the backs of our minds, in a place we did not share, were the lives we had left behind. We kept silent about them as if speaking would be a betrayal of what we now had. I would phone Burton and Gladys for news of Denise, but our life was such a swirl of magic that all news served only to make me feel guilty and selfish.

Michael did not phone home and never wrote to his family. Denise did not leave my thoughts, but she and Michael formed intersecting patterns at the center of my life. While we explored Europe, taking weekend trips or going on tour with the company, Denise was with Martha and John, being formed into the person my family had hoped I would become. I felt the thread that connected us but did not know how far it would stretch in different directions before breaking.

Michael and I pursued our own dreams, propelling ourselves into new countries, new languages, theater, dance, art. Michael found some venues for showing his own choreography. We did showcases of his work, and I toured with the company in Italy and France. I still worked as the administrator, and my life was full of dancing and the business of running a small dance company. Europe embraced us, and I barely noticed that the vision had become more demanding and that I had become less able to dream new dreams of my own.

I began to see our life as a film or piece of theater, and our job became trying to live up to the characters we had created. The film sometimes moved faster than I could keep up with, and it did not seem to have a script which included nurturing my link to my own child or maintaining any ties to Michael's family. We were stretching ourselves further and further from our past.

This rhythm shifted only once, when Burton and Gladys came to visit us. Suddenly my past was in my present, and I was trying to find ways to accommodate both. I hoped that the six years of separation would help Burton and Gladys see me more clearly. Michael had not met them before, so there was the discomfort of a first meeting and their reaction to the reality of his whiteness. They had known from the beginning that I had married a white man, but somehow seeing us together was their first real recognition of it. I also realized during our visit that Michael and I had become very European, and I kept seeing Burton and Gladys as American; their being black seemed secondary to that. Having had no mirror to hold up to ourselves, we were surprised by the changes we had undergone. We commented on things that reminded us of other American tourists, and we were glad to get this meeting out of the way. Thankfully they stayed in a hotel; we met every day to tour the city and have meals together. I was more uncomfortable than Michael, since he had no history with them. He won them over with his charm, his dreams and his announcement that we were thinking of returning to the States.

The remaining tension occurred when they talked about Denise. They heard from John and Martha often, because Denise was having a difficult time. She was very smart but had problems in her interactions with students and teachers. John and Martha had brought home what they considered to be the perfect little girl and given her everything she wanted and needed, expecting her to continue to be their ideal child. I could imagine her listening to the same conversations I had heard when I was her age—everyone deciding what was good for her. I wondered if my presence would be supportive or make it more difficult for her to find her own way. My two lives had met and neither had collapsed; it was clearly time to go home.

We returned to the States in 1976. Michael, wanting to choreograph and perform, formed a company as soon as we returned, and I was his only dancer for the first six months. I kept urging him to audition other dancers until he finally did. I wanted time to take classes, design costumes, and work on finding places to perform.

My life still spanned the ocean. I traveled back and forth from New York to Europe often, working to book other dance companies as well as Michael's. His company had a style of its own. Meanwhile, I was developing a sense of design myself, finding some of the skills I had learned from *Unci* were still in my hands. I was making costumes, sets and props inspired by memories of quill and bead work. I was working as much to define my own creative voice as I was to find venues for Michael's.

In 1979, I landed a commission to design and direct the construction of three sets for a new production in West Berlin. That city welcomed me just as London had, and I worked at the Schaubuhne as production director for a new American work. Berlin was exciting and forbidden at the same time. I listened to the stories of those who had escaped from East Berlin and wondered how much courage I had. But the real thrill was working at art in a setting that was both affluent and supportive. The Schaubuhne was a state-supported theater, and the staff and crew were excellent. Everything I needed was there. It was a real change from working in the small New York theaters where almost everything had to be created from scratch on a shoestring budget. I remembered how Michael's first concert in New York had been performed in a converted warehouse where the dancers helped us sand and paint the floor and sew the curtains.

I was excited by all of the contrasts. The city seemed to live on edge, and I found a place in it easily. I made a lot of friends and found my way around the bureaucracy without too much difficulty. The life of an artist in this city suited my taste. I did not dance much anymore but worked for Michael's company setting up their season in New York and organizing tours when possible. Everyone thought we had a charmed life and a perfect marriage even though we spent a lot of time apart.

On a warm October night I was dressing with particular care and excitement for the opening of the new work. The crew had just finished the set that afternoon. I had been in charge of its design and execution as well as the rest of the production, and I was thrilled to see this opening. We were working on three different sites in the city, and the coordination had been a real challenge for me. I was exhausted, but I wanted to look perfect. Michael was in New York so I was going to the opening with my assistant, Georg. I felt thrilled that the piece was finished, but, as I looked around my apartment, I felt tired and empty, too. This should have been a peak in my career; yet there was no real joy. I had proven to myself and others that I could make miracles happen, and I felt that some of them had merit. But lurking in the shadows was the uneasiness I felt about my own teenage daughter. I wondered if we would ever go to an opening together. We spoke on the phone when I was in the States, and she asked questions about my life and my work, but I knew she had no reference point for the things I was telling her. I wanted her to see what I had done with my life.

Having decided to wear white, I arrived at the theater to meet Georg. I had an old Citroen Deux Cheveux, and, as I got out, the window slammed down on my finger. Blood spurted out on my white shirt. I saw Georg and his girlfriend walking toward me; all of sudden my finger hurt desperately, and I didn't care about the opening. I told them I would take care of the finger, change, and meet them inside. I got back in the car, wrapped my finger in a handkerchief and watched everyone go into the theater. Then I drove slowly through the streets of the city toward my apartment on Schillerstrasse, knowing I would never make it back in time. I went upstairs and lay down on the bed. Looking out the window, I wondered if someday Denise might see an opening. I felt as if I had been speaking someone else's language when I designed this production. I wondered what my own language was. The wound on my finger seemed to be an unconscious flesh offering, just as I would give for *hunbleyca*, crying for a vision. I was crying to learn who I was so that I might bring my voice back to the people. But I was no longer sure who my people were. Perhaps this giveaway from my own body would help my cry be heard, and the vision would come.

My life remained transatlantic, even though Michael stayed most of the time in New York working with his company. I spent almost six months a year in Europe. I kept the apartment on Schillerstrasse and sometimes sublet it while I was in New York. After almost ten years I felt more like a European than an American, and I liked having the contrast in my life. I had moved from dancing to production, hardly noticing the change. Everyone was pleased with my work, and I didn't think to question it. I always arranged to take a few classes and watch rehearsals whenever I could. The rhythm continued, but as the years passed I could not see the charm of our lives so clearly from inside it. To others it looked better each year, but there was a whisper of discontent beginning in my soul. I began to see that what appear to be exciting lives sometimes don't feel that way to those living them.

Denise was now sixteen, and we talked a few times, trying to span the missing years with small talk. I sent clippings from the tours and postcards from Europe home to the family. I had halfheartedly thought of visiting her, but everyone thought it would be too disruptive. So I kept the physical distance between us and tried to bring her back to the forefront of my thoughts. I planned to buy her something really nice for her birthday, since I would be in Germany starting a tour then.

It was 1979, the same year as my commission in Berlin, and I was returning to Germany for a business tour. I left home right after Christmas and arrived in northern Germany during a snowstorm. I had friends in Ahrensburg, a small town not far from Hamburg, so it seemed the perfect place to stay. Since I had to wait out the storm, my friend Gerd Walter decided we might as well have some fun. He hauled his toboggan out and we headed for the woods. There were four of us, and the snow crunched under our feet, breaking the morning silence. The trees were bowed with the weight of the night's snowfall; we appeared to be the first ones out to the hills. We lined up the toboggan and climbed aboard.

On the first run down the hill I was in the middle. I could feel the force of the wind passing my cheeks and the weight of Gerd Walter pressing against me as he leaned into the ride. It was wonderful making that first mark in the snow, and we raced back up to the top of the hill, laughing and making angels beside the path. We saw others standing at the top, disappointed that they had not made the first cuts in the fresh snow. We watched them go down and waited to hear them coming back through the trees before we loaded on again.

On the second ride I sat in the front, because I was the smallest. My legs stretched out in front of me, and I could feel the laughter behind me as we sailed down the hill. There was a small curve ahead through a stand of trees, and we maneuvered it easily. Then suddenly we hit a bump. I thought we would straighten back out and go on down the hill, but the toboggan starting falling over on its side and, carrying everyone's weight, ran over my outstretched leg.

All the others got untangled, but I couldn't get up. It was clear to everyone but me that my right leg was broken, and that I couldn't be moved. As they held a conference about what to do, I looked at my right foot pointing outward and thought, "perfect turnout." After packing snow around my leg, Gerd Walter and one of his friends left to find help. They left Birgit with me. I had seen lots of movies in which someone breaks a leg while skiing and simply spends the rest of the holiday resting at the ski lodge while everyone signs the cast. I knew I'd be on my way in a day or two, with crutches or a cane, shopping for Denise's birthday gift. I lay in the snow thinking all kinds of disconnected thoughts until they came back. The storm had made travel by car impossible, so they had had to find a horse cart that could get into the hills and pick me up for the trip to the hospital.

The cart took me to the clinic in Ahrensburg. It didn't have great facilities, but I was sure they could set my leg and send me on my way. The nurse who came to look at my leg tried to remove my boot so that she could see my ankle. The moment she touched it and tried to lift it off the cot, such pain raced through my body that I lost consciousness. When I came to, I found that they had left on the boot and taken X-rays. The ankle was shattered. I would have to go to the nearest hospital for surgery.

My German was good, but I kept hearing the words without comprehending what they meant. Gerd Walter stayed with me as they put me in an ambulance and drove me to the hospital in Bad Oldesloe. By the time I was undressed and the boot cut off my foot, I realized that I wouldn't be going home tomorrow. I began to understand the conversations with surgeons, doctors and nurses. I didn't let any detail go unexplained once I knew that they were going to operate. The day after I arrived, I had surgery. The storm continued for another week, so I had no visitors.

It was still morning when I regained consciousness and smelled the peppermint tea in a pot next to my bed. No one was in the room, but I kept hearing a buzzing sound like an alarm clock, only duller. I was groggy and kept shaking my head trying to clear it and find out what the sound was. I finally propped myself up on my elbows to try to get some tea. The nurse appeared and held the pot to my lips so I could drink out of the spout. As I coasted back into the mist of sleep, I caught a glimpse of Grandmother Mabel with her arm around Denise, shaking a rattlesnake rattle at me. It was that same buzzing sound. She faded into the sounds and lights of the hospital as I slept through most of the next day.

For two weeks I was alone in the room at Bad Oldesloe, so I asked for paper and started writing. During that time scribbling words down on a page was my only contact with English. I had lots of questions, and the presence of Grandmother Mabel, Denise and the rattle stayed with me. I had time to think about things I had not dared think before. Did I like my life? Was I happy with myself? With my marriage? My work? Was I living my dreams? Was it worth what I had given up? Could I reconnect with my daughter? For many days I just wrote the questions, sometimes only one on a page so that I could see it clearly. Since I didn't have to worry about the nurses reading it, I became engrossed in this inquiry and in the healing of my leg.

When I was released, Gerd Walter picked me up to take me to the airport. The doctors had told me it would be six months before the cast could come off; I had phoned Michael from the hospital with the news. Both of us were concerned about the five-floor walkup to our loft. He decided to meet me in New York at the airport with friends so that we could have some help getting me settled at home. All during the flight back to the States I thought about being dependent on Michael. I couldn't visualize it. Our life had always been the reverse, with Michael being dependent on me. Now, not only would I be isolated because I could not climb those five flights of stairs on my own, but I would have to rely on him for everything else as well.

The first month I wallowed in self-pity. It was January, and New York was ice and slush. Even if I could have negotiated the stairs, the streets were too dangerous for crutches. So I was housebound. It seemed grayer than usual for winter even though I had lots of light from the skylights in the loft. I just kept thinking that this shouldn't have happened to me. I didn't try to do any work and sulked during rehearsals. Then I became angry and difficult. Michael seemed to ignore me and gave most of his attention to the company. He always had a few beers in the evening, but I noticed that sometimes he had six or seven and couldn't stay focused on the rehearsal.

Over time I pulled out the pages I had written in the hospital and occupied myself with answering some of those questions. I began to hear the voices of my childhood—spirits, plants, stories. I could see how I had painted over my own essence, as if with layers of shellac, to protect myself from all the pains of my childhood. So now I began to chip away, one thin piece at a time. At night, memories would play like movies on the ceiling of the loft. I could see and hear my own dreams resurfacing from the deep place where I had hidden them.

I could remember what it felt like to dance just for the pleasure of it. I could even remember dancing at powwows and watching the fringe on the dresses move with the drums and feet. My hands were yearning to make something; I wanted to run them through beads or use them to pull sinew tight. These memories came up through my body to my head and reawakened muscles as well as thoughts.

Over the years Michael and I had merged so totally that neither of us had noticed the loss. Having become the reflection in his artistic eye, I had lost not only the connection with my ancestors and my daughter but with my own artistic vision as well. He had become the artist in isolation, his life buffered by my care of his talent. I had buried my dreams in service to the realization of his. I couldn't remember what it was I wanted, but the desire, now awakened, ached in my chest.

The revelations were painful. The shell of illusion that I had built was shattering just as my ankle had done, and now I was looking for ways to mend it. Michael and I had constructed a life that was woven very tightly around the image we had of ourselves as one dream, one reality. Unraveling that felt like free-falling into an unknown abyss. I dug through my memories of Europe, scouring the landscape for a view of my aspirations. I knew there was something important in that spiritual sleepwalking that I needed to preserve and carry with me. My feeling of flight when I was dancing alone on the stage was connected in some way to the owls of my grandmother's world and were part of the dance of my life. That was real, and the words I sometimes added to the dances in my head to make them mine were real. But most of all, the woman I had grown to be, who could tackle challenges and see herself in many worlds—that was what I had gained. That was what I could pass on to my daughter. I had opened myself through language, and now I had words to speak to her.

Those memories of Europe also brought feelings of remorse and wonder about the separation from my daughter. She had never been there to see me fly. She had never been to one of my performances. A result of the freedom Burton thought he had offered me was that the line between her and me was thin. I hoped the stability and love she had gotten in the bargain were making her strong and happy. Waiting for my leg to heal pushed me to use the language I had found to speak to her. So we talked. In the beginning we approached the conversations with the excitement that is part of finding someone so like oneself. But in our laughter we uncovered the wound of separation. Gingerly we began to speak about it, trying to heal it, too. We came to see that we were as alike as two people could seem. No amount of grooming and sanding could smooth her rough edges; in that she resembled me. Her passion to let her hands speak for her in art and craft were stronger than mine. So was her need to be heard. She was having a difficult time with John and Martha and wanted to come and live with us. That no was the hardest thing I have ever had to say. The thought of her in our life frightened me beyond words, but I tried to continue our conversations so that we would not be suspended in rejection. I knew that Michael and I did not have a home for her; for, while Denise and I were reweaving our relationship, Michael was flailing at ours. The rehearsals became more erratic, and often he drank right through them. The dancers disliked it but were still committed to his brilliance. We all pretended that it wasn't so bad. Even when he came to rehearsals already drunk, we went on as though it were a minor inconvenience. No one dared call it what it was or talk to him about it.

Six months after I returned from surgery, I was told that the leg had not healed properly and would require further surgery. Somehow the pins had been inserted in such a way that, when the bone healed, it was a millimeter shorter than it should have been, which resulted in a cyst forming at the joint. It was clear that I would not dance again. I mourned, but I also knew that dance as we had known it was Michael's language. I was discovering a new one. The dances he made fit his body and his vision. Even when he choreographed for me, it was a limitation of his vision rather than an extension of mine. I always added words and songs to my dances. In secret I would tell the stories of my soul as my feet danced someone else's dream. He created the steps for my body to dance and I added the gestures or words that reminded me of the room under the house where my first healing occurred.

While I sat and searched for my voice, for the things I would say, Michael took care of me and watched as I changed into someone he did not know. Even with his drinking, he was still able to tap into a creative power in almost any medium. He was composing his own music on the synthesizer and had also begun to paint. Our loft was filled with the fury of his creative outbursts. But he didn't seem to see the point in any of it. The ease with which it flowed seemed to diminish its value and his own.

I went back to Berlin for the second operation and stayed in the apartment on Schillerstrasse to recuperate. It was in the center of town and had only one flight of stairs. Friends looked after me well, and I managed to do some freelance work while I was there. It was during those days alone in Berlin that my heart told me I would have to leave my marriage and the life I had built. I had to go so that we both might discover who we were, and because I could not find either of us in the alcoholic haze and the merging of our lives. The people we had created as ourselves were strangling us.

I spent the three months of recuperation working on a script for a performance and thinking about life without Michael. I returned to the States to begin the process of leaving. Michael knew it was happening and numbed himself with alcohol. The last threads of our relationship unraveled. He was so rarely sober that I could not remember the last conversation I had had with the "real Michael." As it all came undone, I seemed to have more room to breathe. I could begin to fill out my body with my soul.

I wrote feverishly, polishing and rewriting the script I had begun in Germany. It was winter again, but this time the gray skies of New York provided me with shelter. I had an urgent need to uncover all of the past I had hidden away. I began with the story of my mother's murder. It had been too long in the dark, and I needed to bring it to light before I brought back my own stories. Something was emerging that I had not seen before, something fragile and unsteady, as my leg had been the first weeks out of the cast. As I was healing physically, I was trying to find my way back into the clan of my grandmother. I remembered my inheritance: "Somebody always singing you." I was not sure where I was going, but I could feel the path being cleared for my footsteps.

The first work, "Victims," was in honor of my mother and was an attempt to understand her. It was all the images and smells and words that I remembered from that time. I didn't even know what name to give it, but I knew it wasn't theater, so I found an apartment to sublet for a month and had the performances there. People came and sat in the living room and watched it unfold. I tried to unravel all the images left of my mother and stepfather from the emotions embedded in me. I repeated a dramatization of my mother's murder, overlaid with staged slide images of my stepfather in the bathroom washing his hands. This took place while I narrated what I remembered of the event and cooked food. I set a table for three and brought out the chicken, potatoes and beans that I had been cooking while speaking. Each time the meal was on the table, the murder was reenacted. This happened three times, until the wall was covered with blood and the table was loaded with food. I invited the audience to share the food so that we were standing in the scene eating together. Those who came from the art world called it performance art, which seemed as good a title as anything. My family was horrified that I would expose our tragedy to the world, but I felt the first wave of love for my mother and the freedom of owning my past. Now I could beckon my daughter to have courage and follow.

My friends did not see the subtle shifts of feeling and thought. They saw the drastic changes in my life: the separation from Michael and the company, the decision to make my own art, of a difficult and personal sort. They were shocked at the change and at the kind of work I had chosen to do. But there was support. Every evening after the performance in that small sublet apartment, people were moved to tell me their stories. A gallery owner even offered to produce the performance in her gallery. I could see a new life starting, but Michael was numb, and he and my friends looked at me with eyes that seemed to say, "You'll never survive this journey." To them Michael and I had seemed like one being or like Siamese twins, for whom separation would be fatal.

chapter six

Iyeska /*mixed*

blood, interpreter

I began the eighties without Michael, struggling to find a new place for myself. I was divided into two parts, each waging war for dominance: She Who Is In Charge, who loved to entertain and perform, and Wolf Girl, the intuitive part of my soul, who was trying to emerge from inside my chest. They pulled me in different directions and led me down different paths. The struggle between them to be heard strained the seams of my reality.

When I moved out of the lower Manhattan loft I had shared with Michael, I wandered from sublet to sublet, looking for some place that would be home to me. This journey led me to Harlem—what the community above 116th Street calls "up south." When I first arrived I was walking in 6/8 time looking for 4/4, trying to fit in. David, a friend of mine who was an artist living in Harlem, showed me a vacant space in a building owned by a friend of his. I was being evicted from my present apartment and needed somewhere to go. He challenged me to take on the space as if it were a grant—no rent for a year if I fixed it up. I wanted a studio which would allow me to spend most of my time making art, so I could find out what I did when I had nothing to do. I said yes to the apartment, and he laughed.

As I stood in the apartment I had taken as a dare, I could see Harlem in its nakedness meeting me in my need. The windows were gone, and the hole in the roof had allowed in enough rain to wash away plaster down to the lath. What had been the bathroom stood as a gaping hole, the copper pipes and fixtures having been ripped out by scavengers long ago. There had been a gate over the window, but it was bent open, framing a wall charred by fire. The smell of water on ash was in every crevice of the place. Fallen plaster crunched under my feet as I looked around, naively imagining this ruin turning into the Salon of Harlem. I had two weeks to make this vision a reality. I envisioned my housewarming as an homage to Bricktop, chanteuse and star of the Harlem Renaissance of the 1920s. I would begin my stay in Harlem with a tribute to one of the bastions of Harlem elegance.

It took much longer than the two weeks to knock down walls, carry plaster in buckets, and scavenge toilets, tile, sheetrock and anything else I needed from the abandoned buildings around me. I managed to impose upon friends to let me sleep on their floors while I worked. But after three months of pushing back the ruin to create a space, and with sixty dollars left, I reclaimed this shell on 121st Street and became part of the neighborhood. There was no need to be anything other than a black person creating something out of nothing. Everyone celebrated that skill. My neighbor, Wendell, who was the unofficial mayor of the street, sat on the front steps or by the corner store with his buddies, commenting on each act of ingenuity that made survival possible—a cart made of two-by-fours with baby carriage wheels or a stash of tile from an abandoned building. He was known as "Big Red," and he welcomed me into the neighborhood by giving me the name "Little Red" for everyone to hear.

I couldn't wait to christen my new home with an event. It already had so much magic from the past and from the strength and endurance of the people who had lived there. I felt honored to be part of the neighborhood. I had handwritten invitations for a "soiree." That evening, 121 candles lit my apartment and the stairway to the roof. The fire escape and the roof were draped in white satin I had found in a dumpster. I still had silver trays from my mother's family, and I used them for serving cucumber sandwiches, a device I had learned from the English as a way of being elegant in poverty.

Acquaintances who waited for just such an occasion when they could deck themselves out in costume finery were asked to bring champagne, which I served with no regret in plastic glasses. My friend Nora, who had a passion for singing torch songs even though she was in a rock band, agreed to perform. My performance was as the impresario and hostess. Nora and I had made a strapless gown from the satin we had left over and created a stage for her on the fire escape so that she could be seen from the floor below. By dusk people were starting to arrive. Word had spread all the way to Soho. Harlem was a new frontier for this kind of performance evening, and by nine the roof and the apartment below were full. Somehow enough champagne arrived for all the guests. Three performers I knew came in tuxedos and acted as waiters for the evening.

When there was barely space for people to stand, I found a place on top of the adjoining roof and offered a toast. As I lowered the glass, Nora appeared on the floor below, singing a capella. The moment was perfect, and my guests fell silent to acknowledge it. Even the folks from the neighborhood were surprised that I had found a white girl who could sing the blues. They also couldn't believe that I wasn't charging people to be there. They kept telling me I could open a great club. The idea interested me briefly, but for the moment She Who Is In Charge was satisfied.

I climbed across the rooftops until I was two buildings away, watching the moment I had orchestrated, because Wolf Girl needed more space. Artists, art dealers, business people, hangers-on—all were up in Harlem to celebrate a black chanteuse from the twenties whose name is hardly ever mentioned. I should have felt at least satisfied, but, as I looked up at the night sky, I wondered if owls ever came to Manhattan. I thought about Grandmother Mabel. I saw no way to bring the comfort of her into my present life or the future. My view of the part of me that had grown out of that life, Wolf Girl, was still trapped inside. The public part of me, She Who Is In Charge, was afraid. She was always uncertain about being in control of things. But she told the story of Wolf Girl's birth to calm us all while we watched the party over the rooftops. Her voice was the voice of a storyteller calling up images from some mysterious and magical world.

I was lying in a shallow stream and I had on a dress that was living. When it got completely wet, it came and sat on my chest like a jellyfish. But I wasn't afraid. Then it filled up with a figure . . . the figure of a girl raised by wolves, like a picture in an old National Geographic. *Her hair was matted and her skin was caked with mud. They came and took her away. They washed her hair, bathed her, soothed her and laid her down in the stream beside me. She looked so peaceful lying there with her eyes closed. But every time she opened her eyes she tried to attack me.*

I waited for the guests to leave, then wandered back to blow out the candles and help Nora out of the strapless creation we had sewn on her. Evidence of the truth of Wolf Girl's story was in my chest as much as remnants of the party lingered in champagne glasses and white satin cloth. I knew the feeling well.

I had been having asthma attacks since right after my mother was killed. I could go for months or even years without having one; then a warning tightness would begin. It was not preceded by sneezing, coughing or any allergic signs. I felt as if I were being squeezed from the inside. The attacks were happening more frequently now, as if to remind me of Wolf Girl's presence. I would be at a restaurant or party and the tightness would begin, like rubber bands tightening around my lungs. The room would shrink, changing from a place full of people, stories and laughter to a space with limited air. I would gasp, trying to fill lungs so tight I could not exhale. And every time I had an attack I tried to pretend that I was fine—that She Who Is In Charge had not lost her grasp on my life. I would find corners where I could spray asthma inhalants into my lungs, trying to coax them into release while no one was watching. It never worked.

I would continue to spray and spray until the lungs no longer responded, when finally my partner, friend or host would realize that I was barely breathing. By then I would be in the full grasp of the attack, able only to ask for a cab to the nearest emergency room. I would leave as inconspicuously as possible and lean back in the cab, focusing all my attention on the in-and-out movements of my lungs. Drivers asking if I was all right were always greeted with "I'm fine."

In the emergency room I would go straight to the person in charge, wheezing out, "asthma attack." I was never denied immediate attention. I went to St. Vincent's in Manhattan so often that they knew me by name and wheeled me right back for treatment. I was familiar with the fluorescent lighting in the hallways and the burning in my brain as I was injected with adrenaline. I knew the drugs, the treatments, and the doctors. But I did not know the girl who was clutching at my lungs. I knew only my fear of her. I would not hear her voice, and I continued to sedate her.

I heard stories of people who had died of asthma attacks, but I believed that something else killed them, although I never followed the line of inquiry as to what that could have been. Often I heard that someone's heart had burst during an asthma attack. I wondered how that was possible and disregarded any notion that it could happen to me. In the hospital, breathing through a respirator, I always made my way back, the drugs pushing me along a well-traveled road. I never stayed overnight. Two or three treatments as I lay under the sterile white lights brought me back from the downward spiral of diminishing air. I never had a tube down my throat or stayed in the emergency room for more than five hours. It was a well-rehearsed dance, in which everyone knew his or her part. The director was She Who Is In Charge.

I found many ways to ease the tension inside through my work. My hands stayed busy making jewelry, costumes and environments for my performance art. My mind was constantly engaged with ideas and texts for performances and the movement of bodies through space.

Since my separation from Michael, I had found a new path and my own voice. We could not completely cut the cord between us, and I persuaded him to perform in some of my work. This relationship ended after a 1984 performance about ourselves, a piece we had created around our love for baseball, "women without air conditioning/man with a fever." It spoke metaphorically about all the signals we had constructed during our marriage. Michael had known all the plays and called them, and I had found my own ways to interpret those calls. As our lives had begun to unravel, we had found new language to negotiate the minefield of our emotions. We invented our own baseball game as a way to find familiarity in the strange place where we were. It seemed to allow us to speak about our parting without pain. Smell had always played a central role in the way I perceive the world, and it was integral to my performance work. In each corner of the space at the museum where we were performing, I placed a vaporizer filled with Vicks, and in the center of the space I built a huge bed covered with a landscape of rumpled white sheets. Michael was at the center of the bed, in pajamas, reciting the names of dead and retired baseball players. I was at the opposite side of the space doing housework (ironing, cooking, snapping beans). The work was orchestrated so that the housework was always set aside by calls of the game. Then we would assume the roles of pitcher and catcher. Eventually a "strike" ended the game, the dialogue and the performance. I thought it was the best work we ever did, and it was the last time we performed together.

Denise and I drifted in and out of touch. Our lives seemed to brush against each other like layers of clothing without ever really touching. We had seen each other a few times at family events such as funerals, and she had married without my knowing it and made me a grandmother soon after. I was a little shocked that I hadn't gotten the news, but I knew our family loved secrets. I was also confused about my position, becoming a grandmother without having experienced being a mother first. When her marriage deteriorated, we began to talk again. We talked about Mom and how we both had fallen into the pattern of her behavior. We talked about the meaning of victimization and about how we fell into that role sometimes. We talked about the family, how they could not see us at all. And out of the talking we decided to spend some time together.

She came to New York in the summer of 1984 and was overwhelmed by the city. I had been seeing photos all along and had always thought she looked just like Mom. What I was not prepared for was the fact that we were mirror images of each other in many ways. We moved our bodies and hands in the same way when we talked, and the rhythm of our speech was the same. She was slim and tall with an elegance I had not imagined. I had known that we looked a little alike, but neither of us was prepared for people being startled by our similarity. Everyone who saw us together commented on it. At first we both found it funny and wonderful; then it became annoying, as if we didn't have our own personalities. In talking about this discomfort some of the old pain came to light. We didn't try to fix it all. We just let it be. There was enough to tackle just getting around the city.

My schedule with rehearsals and work seemed to leave little time for the two of us to be together, but Denise kept saying how glamorous it all was. She was trying to get used to New York in the summer, with all of the people, the noise and ceaseless energy. When she finally felt comfortable enough to take public transportation, she came to see the work I was doing. I was in the middle of rehearsal on a new performance, " . . . and he had six sisters." It was a collage for seven women of orchestrated text based on old wives' tales and folk remedies from the Carolinas, Brooklyn and Harlem. I was thrilled for her to see it and also for her to meet the amazing women who were working with me. She had heard so much from the family about my failures—my lack of financial security and job stability—that I wanted very much for her to see what I considered to be one of my successes.

She stayed for the dress rehearsal and didn't say much, but I felt we had crossed some sort of marker and could go on. It was wonderful for me to see her in the circle of women whom I admired and loved, chatting and talking about her life and her son. We were glad to be together but also glad when the visit came to an end and we could retreat into the rhythms of our own lives.

My work became the center of my life. I created new performances every two or three months, drawing on the demons and treasures from my childhood. I wrote about my stepfather and the time I spent under the house. I connected with people and stories whose struggles resonated with mine. I spent most of the years after separating from Michael trying to understand the dynamics of victims and tyrants by telling my own stories and listening to those of others. I made performances about abortion and about children, about battered women and about men and women in relationships revolving around violence and anger. I always worked on what was sitting on my emotional plate at the moment, trying to make connections with other people and their stories. In between I taught art, or my version of it, to put food on the table. Since London, I had been teaching off and on as a bass line to everything else in my life. I taught movement and theater arts in schools, prisons, nursing homes and universities—wherever there was an opportunity.

My work found a place in the art world, and I was asked to perform and create in exhibitions and performance spaces in New York and around the country. In the spring of 1985 I was on my way to New Orleans to be part of an exhibition at the Contemporary Art Center. I was glad to be going back to Louisiana. I had made a trip there a year earlier with a friend and had been to a show where I saw a landscape painting that affected me, even though I didn't particularly like it. The artist's electric blues and greens were not colors I associated with Louisiana, and the painting stayed with me. When I met Elmore, the artist, on my previous trip, he had talked about riding out in his pickup each day to paint. Since it was winter when I visited and the painting had been done in the spring, I had decided then to come back when I could see what he saw in the landscape.

So when I got the invitation to do an installation and performance in New Orleans, I jumped at it. I also wanted the chance to do a performance I had been working on for over a year, based on the story of Caril Fugate, a woman who had participated in a series of murders in Nebraska. My first solo work, it consisted of a monologue with video and built environment. I hadn't shown it yet and felt the need for some feedback.

It was May and the warm breezes were laden with humidity—a mustiness that only New Orleans can boast—and filled with the smell of chicory coffee and the sound of laughter and music. The undercurrent of African rhythms in the streets and parks, the mystique of voodoo, and the stories from the bayou were all part of the heat of the city. The night I arrived I spent an hour on the phone with Elmore talking about the colors that haunted me in his work. At this time of year I would be able to see the landscape's colors at their peak, so I arranged to rent a car and drive out to his home as soon as I was finished with the performance.

The days I spent rehearsing in the art center were filled with strange waking dreams and desires. At night I would fall into sleep; as the faintest sounds of jazz came from the quarter, my mind would ride on the wisp of sound out into the bayou. The smell of water and heat and the presence of eyes from the past watching and waiting stayed with me during sleep and in waking hours. I would leave the gallery in the middle of the day and wander around the city. I went to the Voodoo Museum and collected things to take to the grave of Marie Laveau, one of the queens of New Orleans voodoo. This brought back dim memories of medicines from Grandmother Mabel. I was pulled by my memories to make offerings to the ancestors buried here. Much time had passed since these thoughts had been in the forefront of my mind, even though they were the fabric of my subconscious.

The night after the performance I went to bed very late. I fell into a deep sleep but woke with a start looking at the clock. It was three in the morning. The full moon was streaming through the window of my room and the realness of my dream would not leave me. I had wandered into a circle of light filled with women from every culture and time imaginable. The light was so brilliant I had to squint in order to see some of their faces. They were all sitting cross-legged on the ground. My eyes were drawn to the woman immediately across from me. I could see every detail of her clothing and the part in her hair. But most of all I could see her lips—full, slightly open and encrusted with tiny beads of pearl and turquoise. As much as I wanted to look around, I could not take my eyes off her lips; she moved across the circle and kissed me. I woke up with the feeling of the stones still on my lips. In flashes during the next day I could still feel those lips touching mine.

The performance went well. I packed my bags and headed across Lake Pontchartrain on my way to Lafayette. Elmore was meeting me at Mulatte's in Lafayette to lead the way to his home. Of course, we stopped to see friends and eat first. The drive to his house took us deeper into Cajun country, along the levee, past houseboats and docks where the cypresses and their shadows in the water seemed the only inhabitants. Now I was moving into a world where memories of the songs and dances from the ancestors still lived, where dancing, singing and playing music are a strong link to the past and to the land. Everybody there does some of all three as well as cook good Cajun food.

The driveway greeted us and led us a full mile winding through the bright green fields toward a house and an Airstream trailer in the front yard. That trailer was to be my guest quarters. After I had put my things away, we ate dinner, and Elmore's wife, Ann, wove stories of *traiteurs*, healers/herb and root doctors. She had grown up in Haiti, and, even though she didn't speak much about it, I felt she had deep feelings for the medicines of voodoo. Before we went to bed they unfolded their plan of a trip the next day to introduce me to some of the Cajun music families near them and to show me the prairies of Elmore's paintings.

That night I heard animals rummaging outside the trailer as I was falling asleep. I wanted to get up and look outside but I was too tired, and dreams were pulling me deeper into sleep. At first I thought I was outside the trailer, but then I knew I was in a dream with a woman standing alone waist-deep in the bayou. I thought it was another cypress, but she began to sway and sing in French in a kind of toneless voice. I couldn't remember much of the song except the first two words, "*mon colonel.*" When I asked in the morning about the noises, I was told they were made by havelinas and was shown a long orange tooth like a beaver's. I still didn't know what they looked like, but it was good to be back in a land where animals weren't afraid to come right up to the house.

Beginning early, the next day was filled with the playing of music and the consuming of food, activities that held families and this place together and seeped into every pore of the landscape. We were going to start by going to Fred's Lounge in Mamou for the early morning music, but we got sidetracked and ended up at the home of the Ardoins, some of the best Cajun musicians around. I had seen Bois Sec Ardoin in New York and was ecstatic at being able to meet him and his family. We arrived at lunch time, and the pots were full of crawfish etouffee. We hadn't been in the house five minutes before the plates were on the table and we were sitting down to share food and stories. We spent the afternoon looking at family albums, touring the grounds, and meeting all the children, grandchildren and great-grandchildren.

It was twilight as we began the journey home; almost as an afterthought, Elmore decided to take me to see Tante Inez. She was one of the last a capella Cajun singers and had lots of stories to tell. When we arrived at her little white frame house, her nephew greeted us on the porch and then went inside to tell her there was company. We waited on the porch as we heard her preparing to come outside. She appeared wearing a housedress, her gray hair wrapped into a bun on the top of her head. Laughing as she came through the door, she grabbed Elmore and squeezed him till he turned red, then did the same with Ann. She came and stood in front of me with a frown of concentration which made me very uncomfortable. "You speak French?" she asked before saying hello. I murmured that I had learned to speak French in school and had lived in Paris for a while. "Oh, you speak that dummy French," she said, as she motioned us inside.

The living room was a shrine—altars in every corner with flowers and mirrors and candles. After some pleasantries and inquiries about her family, Elmore asked her to sing for us. Before she started she leaned back in her chair and said, "When I was small everyone said I couldn't sing too good. But I sang anyway, all the time, because I liked to sing. So I just kept on singing, even now." Then she closed her eyes and began, "*Mon colonel . . .*" I was in shock. I still don't remember the rest of the words of that song. The woman in the dream did not look like Tante Inez, but the voice was hers and it was the same song.

When she finished, Elmore said that we should be getting on home. She stood up and went over by the mantelpiece and pointed at me with her eyes and chin, saying, "Leave her here. Bring some clothes tomorrow, then come back for her in a few weeks. We've got some workin' to do." I couldn't even protest about my rental car and the need to get back home; anything I had planned to do seemed to disappear in her determination. I was frightened, but I was also very secure in my knowing that she was right. I was only frightened of myself and my own feelings.

Tante Inez had a biting sense of humor and elected to call me "dummy" during my entire stay. The first night was spent with songs.

She tested my French by trying to teach me songs from her mother and grandmother. She laughed heartily at my mistakes. My brain was spinning by the time she gave me blankets and pillows for the couch in the living room. She kept the door to her bedroom closed and I could not even get a peek inside. Among all the candles and altars, I felt that I was sleeping in a shrine.

It was still dark when Tante Inez shook me awake the next morning. I couldn't remember where I was until I heard "*Ça va?*" It was hard to switch from the English in my dreams to French, but the language helped place me in this strange landscape with a guide who had chosen me. I got up and followed her closely as she went out of the house and down the road. I had had time enough to put my shoes on and was hoping that my sweat suit would be okay for the morning air. We kept on walking, with the light changing, until we finally reached the water.

Stretching into the water was a rotting dock which looked as if it could bear no weight, but Tante Inez stepped onto it with confidence and motioned me to follow. She sat down, and I did the same; the wood was cold and moist against my body. Looking at me so hard I felt that she could see through me, she said, "*Pacquette de Kongo.* Kongo medicine, that's what you came here to learn. You must open old doors to hear and you must bring back your owl sight to see." I began shivering, not from the cold and damp but from the knowingness of her. I could feel Wolf Girl prowling in my chest. She was guiding me on the road to my African ancestors, which I knew would also lead me back to Grandmother Mabel.

We spent weeks roaming the landscape looking for roots and herbs and singing the songs which would coax them and their medicine into view. I had trouble with the idiomatic French, which gave her many occasions to burst into waves of laughter. We entertained ourselves taking Polaroids of each other, and she took it upon herself to pose me in front of different altars in the house. I thought then that it was a game, but I know now that those photos kept me with her and under her protection. Each day passed quickly and opened new teachings for me. And each day was connected to the next by music and by the smell of cayenne pepper being stirred into simmering pots.

Near the end of the third week, I was allowed into her bedroom. A carved four-poster bed and a large oak closet filled the room. There was barely space to move around the bed or open the door to the closet. On top of the closet a few candles were arranged, and photos formed a halo on the wall at the head of the bed. We had run out of film for the camera, so she called out the window for her nephew, who was never very far away, to go to the store and get more. I fished the money out of my purse while she began digging in the closet, pulling out boxes of jewelry and photographs. When the bed was covered, she finally found what she was looking for—a shoe box containing odds and ends of jewelry. She picked out something and placed it in my hand. It was a pair of earrings encrusted with tiny beads of pearl and turquoise. I put them to my lips and she laughed.

One morning, as I was sorting out plants we had picked to hang for drying, I saw Elmore's car drive up. I realized I had been there a month. He waved to me, then hauled a large pot out of the back seat. I waved back and went in the house to prepare for a feast. I could hear Tante Inez and Elmore laughing as I covered the kitchen table with an oilcloth, which reminded me of Pine Ridge and Grandmother Mabel. "Are you ready to go back to civilization?" he hollered as he brought the huge pot of gumbo in and put it on the stove. "I returned your rental car. We'll take you back into New Orleans to the airport." I realized I hadn't thought of such matters in the entire month I had been there. It had been a long stay, and a feeling of restlessness had begun in my chest the night before. I heard whispering in my sleep. Tante Inez had sung a song for the wolf that morning at sunrise, and I knew it would soon be time to leave. We all ate and laughed and sang, and I wore my new earrings. Then I packed my things into a brown paper bag, and we stood beside the car and took the last photos.

In the Airstream at Elmore's that night I lay awake trying to remember all the plants and songs and recipes. I finally fell asleep to the sound of Tante Inez's voice singing me a one-word lullaby—*malembé*—a word she said her ancestors brought from Africa. But even in my sleep She Who Is In Charge was trying to quiet the rising voice of Wolf Girl as she spoke to me in my dreams. She continued her story so that Wolf Girl could not speak.

She preoccupies me, this Wolf Girl. Whenever I stop for a moment I see her lying in the stream, waiting. One day a friend asked to see her. The sound of Wolf Girl's scream, as she opened her eyes and sprang forward trying to bite, came from some place inside me that didn't need my throat. That sound leapt into the air and stayed there while I dragged her back to the stream and laid her down. My friend had seen her, and it took a day to scrape the scream out of the air. So I've made a pact, a contract signed in blood. I've built her a beautiful room with a waterfall. I think it is over, but some remnants of her birth stay in my chest, making it difficult to breathe.

The time with Tante Inez had made Wolf Girl stronger, and I could feel her stalking the edges of my life. I returned to New York knowing that the truce was not working. But I had no solutions, so I just kept on with my life, the performances, the visits to the emergency room. One thing had changed. There was a lot more humor in my work. I had learned from Tante Inez to laugh at myself, and my performances were lighter. I even did a country-western revue and wrote a few songs for it. I created a black female country-western singer character named Shirlene. It was a relief, and it was also a good stretch for me as a performer.

A few months later the fight was reaching its peak. I was in the emergency room two to three times a week. Then one morning, having returned home from the hospital late the night before, I found myself standing in my studio and looking out the window to the fire escape of my Harlem apartment. I could see the fake window shade paintings on the abandoned building across the street. Hardly able to breathe, I was trying to reach the phone. I knew I had to call for help, but who? My attention shifted to the exposed lath on the wall I was replastering. I wondered if they measured the distance between each small piece of wood. Then I remembered I had to call for help, but I couldn't make my hands reach for the phone. I was still wondering about that as I crumpled to the ground, gasping for air.

In a sudden shift I was outside the window looking at myself lying on the floor. I knew I was dying, and kept saying it to myself: "I'm dying." But it seemed only a moment later when the door burst open and two men in white uniforms came into the apartment with a stretcher. I watched as they bent over me with an oxygen mask; from my place on the fire escape I could see my downstairs neighbor's entire family crowded into the doorway. "Let's move. I don't think she's gonna make it" was what I heard as the men lifted me onto the stretcher. From the fire escape I was saying to them, "I'm dying."

They moved the people out of the doorway as they carried me on the stretcher down the stairs. I cut right through the building with my eyes and watched them carry me out to an ambulance. Someone in the street asked, "Which hospital?" It didn't really matter anymore. I could breathe all right from where I was watching, but I wasn't breathing at all in the ambulance.

The ambulance faded away beneath me, and I found myself on an escalator that had no steps. There was no landscape, only light the color of corn pollen, and it was brilliant. As I moved along, the light became even brighter and changed from golden to white. I saw Grandmother Mabel in front of me holding out her arms. She was dressed as she was next to my grandfather in the picture on the wall of her house, and, as I got closer, I realized that she was also as young as she appeared in the photograph. She motioned for me to come next to her; I was surprised that I didn't have to walk to get closer. Then I saw the circle of women, the same one I had seen in my dream in Louisiana.

This time they weren't seated. The women were standing inside beams of rainbow light. They were women from every place and every time. Grandmother Mabel took my hand and led me inside the circle to stand beside her. Across from me was a Chinese woman with bound feet. Her head was bowed, but she looked up at me and I stared into her eyes and at the patterns of shifting light on her silk brocade jacket. Someone took my other hand and I looked over to see an African woman dressed in white, with a white headwrap and white clay painted across her eyes like a mask. All the women were holding hands now. The light was blinding and I closed my eyes. Everyone started to sit down. As I began to sink to the ground, Grandmother Mabel took my arm firmly and led me out of the circle.

I was back on the escalator and she was waving to me. "We are always here for you," she said. "Now go back. It's not time for you." I moved away from the light and circle. As the light became more distant, I began to hear sounds of feet moving on tile and the hum of quiet motors as the light changed from white back to the corn-pollen gold I remembered. I was settling into the golden glow when suddenly my eyes opened and I saw a fluorescent light overhead. I shook my head to make sure I was conscious and saw a man standing over me in white. I thought he might know the African woman I had seen, but when I saw a name badge on his jacket—Clemens D.D.S.—I thought, "My God, a dentist saved my life."

He examined me and asked me questions, then pulled the curtain around my cubicle. For the first time I could hear a whispering in my thoughts that I knew was the voice of Wolf Girl, strong and clear. Now she could tell the story of her coming in her own way. Her voice was sharp and quick almost like a panting.

It was as quick as a thought. I didn't feel my body move. I could hear my family howling in the distance but I could not see them. I was shifted to a shallow stream. I was frantic, struggling to return to what I knew. Hands caressed me. Voices soothed me. I closed my eyes and drifted into the mist. Every time I opened my eyes I panicked. I knew they were stealing my scent. The sound of my wolves faded into the distance. I tried to bite but the power of their touch and the hum of their voices pulled me back into the mist. I floated in the stream next to her. I knew she had called me here. So I listened to her, felt her and let myself merge with her.

Another lapse into the golden light, and my eyes opened to see an owl staring at me. I was in complete darkness except for the owl's illumination by moonlight. It opened its wings and then came to rest again as I focused my eyes and realized it was a painting on the wall across the room. With this realization came an awareness of my body— tubes up my nose and needles in my arm. I could hear the respirator and see the pump going up and down. I wasn't quite sure what it had to do with me. I started grabbing at the tubes as someone came to the side of the bed.

It was the night nurse assuring me that I should lie quietly and try to sleep. As I listened to her I became aware of other sounds in the room. I looked around and saw that I was in a room like a dormitory with many beds. I could hear moans, groans and words scattered in the night. I asked the nurse where I was. "Geriatrics ward at St. Luke's. There wasn't any other space. They'll try to move you soon. Now just rest."

All night these old women cried out for help, for the nurse, for God. I tried to block it out and kept asking when I would be moved. The doctor came the next morning and told me how lucky I was. " We thought we had lost you," he said. "We had no vital signs for a couple of minutes." It didn't seem quite real, since I thought if I had survived death I should be able to get up and go home now. But after my first attempt to take out the tubes, I found no more strength to move any part of my body. I was attached to machines, and there were no other free beds in the hospital. Since I was there, I began to listen.

The grandmothers' voices rumbled over each other day and night. From every bed in the ward came the sounds of their journeys. It could have been delirium, but I listened as if they were telling oral histories,

stories of their walks toward death and their returns from it. They were riding that same escalator I had ridden, and it soothed me to know I was with fellow travelers.

Like a chorus in call and response, it went on day and night in the ward. One voice would begin: "Of course dead people can talk. I'm dead. I'm talkin'. If I wasn't dead I wouldn't be talkin' to you." And as that voice faded in exhaustion, another would find its way in the room. "I've got plenty money. I'll give you two hundred dollars if you just call the police and ask them to tell me where I am and who these people in these beds are. I hear people talkin' but they're whisperin', trying to keep me from hearin'. They're so mean to me 'cause I'm old and blind. They're talkin' even when I'm tryin' to sleep but I can't make out what they're sayin'. I know they're talkin' about me and tryin' to keep it a secret. Take all my money. Just call someone and ask them to tell me where I am." All night long these pleas and questions and stories would echo through the ward, and I learned to let them flow along and even to be thankful for them.

I went home two weeks later. It was the end of August in 1986. Even the mugginess of a New York summer could not dampen my joy at being home. Friends had cleaned the apartment and moved things around to make it easier for me. They had taken away anything that could have collected too much dust, as we were all pretending that this illness was caused by allergies. No one mentioned the Wolf Girl growing in my chest. I wondered if they knew.

I moved around the apartment touching everything—the altars for each of the directions, the walls I had plastered myself, even the metal bars on the windows facing the abandoned building in the back. The blue patterned cloth on the couch and the peach of the tile seemed alive with light. And I kept looking at myself in the mirror. I was transparent, and the quiet voice of Wolf Girl was whispering inside me.

I use her eyes to see before the smell and sound of things assault me. I wait motionless, watching, so I can move, speak and eat as she does . . . She

Who Is In Charge. The memory of the other seeing, smelling and hearing still haunts me. The simplicity of instinct lurks in my dreams and out of the corners of my eyes.

My old thoughts and this new voice rang inside my transparent body and emerged as an incredible joy at being here on earth. I "tasted" miso soup and chocolate mousse. I "felt" the cold of the tile floor as I put my feet out of bed. This joy streamed from my hands in rays of light. I could pass it on to people I was with. It was palpable. People came by the house to be touched. This joy and power flowed through me for a month. All this time I could see Grandmother Mabel in the apartment with me.

Sleeping and eating little during this time, I sat and listened to Grandmother Mabel during the days when I was alone. She filled me again with stories of plants, stones and spirits. We journeyed often with the owls on the pathways to the dead. I sat with my mother and made peace with my stepfather. And I came back to this Earthwalk more joyful each time.

I found new ways to talk to Denise. She had been frightened by my near death and the possible loss of her link to the past. I phoned her from the hospital and when I got home. I didn't tell her of Grandmother Mabel's presence, but I passed things on to her that I had been clutching in secrecy for too long. I wanted her to feel the connection we had to our ancestors through the stories and through the earth.

It did not last long, this time of being in both worlds, but it brought my past into the present and it allowed Wolf Girl and She Who Is In Charge to exist harmoniously within me. The war was finished on the day when Grandmother Mabel did not come to teach me. Wolf Girl told me, *We called a truce. We will not fight. Silently we have been looking for openings. I found that I could walk through passages of fear and doubt hidden in her. She could sneak up on me through laughter, a sound I did not know. In these moments I ran wildly through the tunnels of her soul looking for my way home. She was doing the same. Exhausted we slept together. Now we see and speak in duet—not the same voice or the same eyes but harmonized, two views at once.*

That was the last I heard their voices and the last of my trips to the emergency room. Now the conversation with Denise began in earnest.

One Sunday afternoon not long after I had heard the voice, I sat with the phone pressed to my ear and felt as if I were talking to my daughter for the first time. I could feel and hear the person she had grown to be—a woman and a mother. I wasn't talking to a child any longer, and I could not hold any preconceived pictures of her in my mind. She was teaching me about constancy in spite of how long the spaces were between our calls and visits. Through her love I found joy in my grandson without feeling his birth as a theft of my own youth. I could also see myself in her.

It had taken a long time to come to this place. The journey had taken place along many intersecting roads rather than on one straight one. Perhaps the fact that we are much alike had made it necessary to keep our distance. Even our memories had been held at arm's length until now. We had spent years making our way through the cobwebs of everyone else's opinion of us so that we could come to know each other in our own way. I listened to her stories of daily life and saw her walking through it with elegance and pain. In the Sunday afternoon sunlight we laughed about nothing and stayed on the phone even through the silences.

Cangleska
Wakan /*sacred hoop*

My health returned, and I went back to my work. I was performing and creating more than ever, but I had begun to find New York lacking. It was 1988, the decade was coming to a close, and I began to think about leaving the city. I would miss my friends, but I had an intense yearning to be close to the earth, to dirt, as I had been in the basement of my grandparents' house. I took a short vacation to Arizona and fell in love with the desert—the space, the colors, the dry air—but I wasn't sure if that was the place where I wanted to live. I returned to New York and waited for a sign. When none came that seemed prophetic enough, I decided to leave anyway.

I had chosen Arizona as a destination simply because I had been there and liked it, but, just before I left New York, I remembered staying in a guest house in Pilar, New Mexico, with a friend. I decided to change my plans and go there, so that I could rest and consider what to do. When I called Pat, the woman who owned the guest house, she told me I could stay a month for $150 because it was the winter. So I made my reservation, packed my truck with everything I might need for a few months, and headed out, thinking I was taking a short break.

I had bought a new Dodge Dakota pickup, and it felt like this was the maiden voyage for us both.

I settled into Pilar in the beginning of 1989 and enjoyed the winter as if I had always lived in New Mexico. The village was built into the banks of the Rio Grande River at the bottom of the gorge. It was a small collection of adobe houses which looked as if they had been carved into the gorge. I never met any of the other residents, but I was sure they knew I was there.

In the winter the sun lit up the middle of the gorge and then moved across the edges so that only the mesa above was lit. Towards the end of the day, as the light moved across the river, it would turn the water a powdery blue color, which before I had thought only happened in bad cowboy art. Some days I would follow the sun to the top of the gorge and lay a blanket out on the rocks for an afternoon nap in sun and snow. Other days I would climb around the lava rocks of the gorge looking for treasure, for new materials that I could shape into images from my dreams. I found branches of sage weathered from the sun and skeletons of cholla cactus which I painted and beaded and then gave back to the mesa. The river was strong in my life and the spirits of that water whispered to me in the night and came to my door seeking entry. I wasn't scared, but I knew that I was in a place of great power, and that I should respect and honor that.

I didn't try to make any friends or meet local people, because I kept telling myself I would be leaving soon. But after three months of saying that, it was clear that I would not be leaving New Mexico yet. In those months I had barely spoken to any other people. I had become so shy that I would wait outside the post office until the mailbox room was empty, so I would not have to say hello to anyone during my infrequent trips to town.

I did make friends with the night creatures and the animals of the land: coyote, lizard, snake and rabbit. I began making art from the cholla cactus and sagebrush as well as from bones and rusted metal that I found on my walks. I called them spirit sticks because they conjured up and honored the spirit of the land for me. As spring came I lay on the mesa more and more each day in the sunlight, watching ants on the anthills and the trails of lizards in the sand. This time of gathering and making wedded me to the landscape of northern New Mexico; it felt like home. But I knew that Pilar would fill with life when the snow melted in the mountains and came rushing down the river calling to the white water rafters from all over the country. I didn't relish the idea of living on the bank of the river during that time. I decided to move.

Taos was the nearest town, so I bought the newspaper and looked for a place. I took the first thing I found for rent and spent that spring and part of summer in a trailer park in Llana Quemado as the only "gringo" there. I went back to New York only once, to pick up the rest of my belongings, then sent out a postcard with my "permanent" New Mexico post office box address to everyone in my address book. I knew I wouldn't be in the trailer park forever but I wanted to stay near the gorge and Taos Mountain so I figured the address would be good anywhere I went.

I drove all around looking for a place to winter. In July I realized that I was going to Tres Piedras every week just for the view of Taos Mountain and the other mountain ranges. The town wasn't much more than a gas station, diner and post office, but it had a 360 degree view of the mountains that was breathtaking. Everyone told me that it also had the worst winters because it was at 8200 feet, but I wasn't disheartened. I kept going to the general store asking about places to live until they finally told me about a log cabin that might be available.

I decided that this was where I wanted to be for the beginning of the new decade, cajoled the owner into renting the cabin to me, and settled in. It was one of the first buildings in Tres Piedras, having been built one hundred years ago by a forest ranger and added to over the years by his family and other tenants. There had been no method to the building of the additions, so the house looked disjointed. The original cabin was beautiful, with its hand-scraped vigas, but the rest of the house was badly insulated and I knew would be difficult to heat.

I prepared for the last winter of the eighties by stacking ten cords of firewood that had been delivered. I was trying to make the primitive cabin resemble a home more than a survival hut. It was July so I had some time, but the nights were already beginning to have a hint of the cold that was coming. That high up in the mountains, winter chill starts very early. I knew that by August I would need a fire in the evening.

When the sun set, the sky would fill with lavenders and peach tones. I always wanted to lie in my hammock during that time so that I wouldn't miss a moment of it. On July 17, I had just settled into the gentle swing when I heard the phone. I was keeping one ear attuned to it because Denise was expecting again and was due to deliver any day. When I answered, I knew it would be about the baby. Martha said, "Denise just had a baby girl," and I let out a real trill. I know it shocked her, but she didn't acknowledge it. Neither of us was exactly comfortable with our roles as Denise's two mothers. But I owed her respect for having raised my daughter, and she returned the feeling for my having given Denise life. We exchanged some other pleasantries, I said "thanks," and we hung up.

I collected the things that I still had from Grandmother Mabel and took them outside. Sitting on the ground, I spread out the bundles of stones, feathers and other objects she had given me. I sang songs that I remembered from her or had learned from other grandmothers. I wanted the link between us to be strong so that she could touch the child of my dreaming with her spirit. I sang the songs into the setting sun and began making the pouch for my granddaughter. The next day at sunrise I would go to make offerings and pray for a name for this granddaughter and sing her into our family. There was a special place I had found at the lip of the gorge which had given me strength many times in my transition from city life. It was the place where the spirit could soar and touch the skies. So I planned to go there in the morning. It was dark when I finished singing. I brought everything inside and packed up the things I would need the next day.

I got up just as the sky filled with a hint of sunrise behind Taos Mountain, packed the pickup and headed out for the gorge. As I drove, the sun moved over the mountain till the gorge was washed golden in its light. I parked the truck in a spot off the dirt road where it wouldn't be immediately seen and walked off toward the edge of the gorge with my bundle. The rocks were deep purple, accented by brilliant celery-green lichen and silvery sage. I found a hidden place in an arroyo which could not be seen from the winding gorge road or the high mesa. The bed of the arroyo was a lava flow cutting through sand where the tracks of the night creatures could still be seen. I added my footprints to theirs. A juniper tree which had forced its way through the lava and sand was at the center of the arroyo overlooking the gorge. Each rock on the ground at my feet seemed like a perfect sculpture. I resisted the urge to impose my presence on the place by arranging them.

I sat very still and watched the sun rise in the sky. When it was overhead I stood up. This was the sun of no shadows and it was worth waiting for. Everything was naked in its light, revealing truth to those with courage enough to look. I had come here often and slept under the juniper or watched the shadows of eagles and ravens on the rocks. Now I returned to pray for the dreaming of our family. I had come to call to the eagles. This was the one place on the mesa where golden eagles soared on the currents created by this giant cut in the land. I faced east, toward the sacred mountain of Taos. The sun forced me to squint until my eyes were slits searching the sky for the *wanbli oyate*, the eagle nation. My mouth was parched now, but I did not want to be disturbed by the thought of my thirst, or even by the thought that I had brought only enough water for an offering with dried meat, corn and berries.

The wind was strong even in my sheltered spot; it was the only sound whistling through the gorge. Since there were no birds circling in the sky, I waited and called to the spirits of the four winds for my granddaughter. I asked for her name to be whispered to me so that I might carry it to her. I laid out four wooden bowls on the perfectly shaped rocks and filled them with water, corn, meat and berries. With the filling of each bowl I asked for the eagle nation to bring a sign for her. I knew she was strong, because the wind was strong and clear, and I knew she came from my dreams as I had come from the dreams of Grandmother Mabel. While I was swinging in the hammock and watching the sky before the phone call came, I had felt her birth like a fullness in my heart. I had felt her presence connecting us both to the grandmothers.

I closed my eyes and saw Grandmother Mabel standing at the rim of the gorge framed by the sky and Taos Mountain. She was singing in a whisper. I could not understand her at first, but she kept singing, the words gliding on the wind. Then I heard "*tate heta, tate heta*" ("wind in the mountains"). I knew that was to be the baby's name. I opened my eyes, sure that Grandmother Mabel would still be there. But in the blue sky over the gorge floated a solitary golden eagle riding on the currents of the wind. I did not need to squint; the sun had moved. My eyes followed the eagle until it disappeared above the reach of my sight. I left the bowls and offerings with other giveaways for the name that had been brought. I walked slowly back to the truck with her name in my heart.

On the drive back home I remembered my inheritance: "You, going/coming back being. Don't talk so much coming back. Makes going clear and coming back stronger. Grandmothers always singing you going. Grandchildren always singing you coming back. Somebody always singing you, going/coming back being."

I had been led to this place, to the life I had here in New Mexico, and to my new relationship with my daughter through the singing presence of my grandmother. Now I would have the first songs of my granddaughter, her laughter, and her search for language as my new guideposts. I wondered if Grandmother Mabel knew how long it was taking me to understand the gift she had given me in those words.

As soon as I returned home, I packed up the pouch I had made for my granddaughter, along with some of the things Grandmother Mabel had given me. As I prepared to close the box and phone my daughter to tell her it was on its way, I thought of my grandson, born almost six years earlier with no name and no acknowledgment from his grandmother, and I started to cry. I didn't have words to tell him the sorrow I felt over this, and I could not retrieve the years, but I could reach out to him with the same love I had for Wind in the Mountains. I carefully divided my treasures from Grandmother Mabel and spent the rest of the day making him a pouch. I felt his name would come to him on its own, but I needed to embrace him finally in my lineage.

I sat with their pouches under the desert sky for four days; then I phoned Denise. She cried, too, when I told her about the box and what was in it. She had given the baby an everyday name, but she was pleased for her to have a family name that connected us all. As we were talking, both of us speaking through our tears, I looked out the window and could see, high over the mesa, a golden eagle circling and floating. I told her about it, not sure if she would know how much it was a part of our conversation.

I settled into a kind of peace after that, continuing to stack wood for the winter and find inspiration and solace in sunrises and sunsets. A few weeks later I had a dream. I was up at Four Corners, one minute looking up at Shiprock, the next leaning against it with the shape of the stones impressed in my back. The sun had set, but the sky still held impressions of its passing in lavenders and pinks. A crescent moon hung over the flat landscape, which was becoming a sheet of darkness. Even the smell of the dry desert air filled my nose. I woke up suddenly, the feeling of the rock against my body so real I was surprised to find myself still at home. I knew I had to go there and lie on those rocks to find out the message of the dream.

It took a week for me to act. I kept putting it off even though I had nothing better to do. I split logs and gathered treasures in the desert till I was faced with nothing but the dream in view. So I packed the car and took off toward Four Corners. I still wasn't sure why I was going except that I wanted to put my body against that rock just as I had in the dream. During the drive I kept drifting in my thoughts back to my grandchildren and their life among relatives whom I had not seen in years. I drove slowly and didn't arrive till the afternoon.

The weather was full of summer storm energy—bolts of lightning in the sky and fast-moving clouds. The main road cut through the tail of the formation, and at first I was frustrated at the thought of not being able to get to the height of the rock as I had in my dream. Then I saw a white Jeep turning off onto an almost imperceptible dirt road along the formation. Pressure built in my head as if I were entering some strong electromagnetic field; I felt that it might burst. I kept trying to pop my ears. I seemed to be driving in slow motion. I had been following the Jeep, but I was moving so slowly that I met it headed back down from the peak. As we crossed paths at the bottom of the rock, a family of Navajo smiled and waved me on up the road. I drove to the base of the spire and got out. I felt as if time had stopped.

In all of the horizon before me there was only one hogan visible, and it was so far away that it was barely recognizable. Lightning filled the sky behind it. Now the pressure was gone. I thanked whoever lived in that hogan for guarding this sacred place, and I brought out tobacco and sweetgrass as gifts in thanksgiving. On a rock at the base of the peak, I laid out stones, bones and feathers from my own bundle. The thunder became music for the ritual of my being there.

The wind came in streams; one wave picked up a feather and blew it upward in a spiral, then gently laid it back down with my things. Trying to frame some questions, I picked up the bones, and they leapt from my hand. There were no questions, only directives, if I could be still enough to hear them. As the feather landed back on the rock, a flock of birds, which had looked like shadows, soared together soundlessly in a spiral through the peaks of the rock, then disappeared. I left the things on the ground and crawled up to the rock, lay on it and closed my eyes.

As my body touched the rock, my mind opened like a kaleidoscope. My view widened and shifted to connect me to this protrusion from the earth. Even though it thrust out of the earth, I felt it like a mother standing behind me, rooted in the rock of the ground supporting me. I perceived the most powerful feminine energy I had ever imagined. It was not images that occurred in this opening but fusion with a force. I knew then that this place was not called Shiprock by the people who cared for it.

As I opened my eyes and looked at the rock and its shape, the inspiration and origin of all built form came into question for me. In that moment, in a landscape where nothing can hide, all the power of First Woman came in to inhabit this form I was lying on, pushed up out of the ground by some immense thrust in nature. I was connected through this shape touching my body to memories of moonlodges, menstrual huts, the temple of the vestal virgins in ancient Rome and all other shapes, natural and made, that held the teachings and secrets of women through time. I received viscerally a knowledge of the origin of these places that had nothing to do with a history constructed piecemeal from fragments of times past. That moment altered not only the way I was to view dwellings, artifacts, symbols and ritual but also the movement of bodies in space and the feminine form in particular.

This connection went beyond my bond with Grandmother Mabel. Through her teaching and her care, my body had been prepared to experience the birthplace of our knowing, the Earth. As this thought ran through my mind, lightning began to slash the sky like an exclamation point. The energy that filled me was so great that I could not continue to lie still, and I made my way back to the truck. The stormy sky pressed on me as I picked up my things and left my offerings.

Just as I started the truck, it began to mist, but there was no pressure in the air. The sky was pink with sheets of lightning. I thought I had been at the rock for ages but could see from the clock that it had only been an hour. The ride back to the main road was shorter than I remembered, and the mist had become a steady drizzle by the time I got there. I was headed for Farmington to spend the night when I saw a rainbow ahead. Thinking that a pot of gold at the end of a rainbow was an appropriate ending to the day, I smiled to myself.

The truck glided on and was filled with a continuing sequential mist of colors—purples, blues, greens, reds, oranges. I gasped as I saw the colors pass over my skin, tinting me. Then it was over. I stopped the truck and got out, staring at where I had just been and saying out loud, "*I just drove through a rainbow.*" Then I got back into the truck, drove straight for Farmington and checked into a motel. I found out from one of the locals that the Navajo call that formation Rock with Wings. I wondered if in their own language those words had other meanings. Sitting in my motel room, I felt as if I had been touched by the movement of those wings, as if they had swept over me into the heart of that rainbow. Those wings had erased everything but the connection through Grandmother Mabel to the earth and her multicolored power.

I had my own inheritance to pass on to my granddaughter now. I didn't have words for it yet, but I had a place to start. I phoned Denise from the motel and could hear Wind in the Mountains in the background crying. It was a joyous sound, a reaffirmation of her presence in our lives. I lay back on the bed and began to search for the words I would use to tell her the story of the women who had dreamt her.

chapter eight

Dancing between the Worlds

Like Grandmother Mabel I want my granddaughter to remember every-thing I do, but, even as I tell the story, I find myself pulling out the strands of strongest connection. It is not that one fact has more truth than another but rather that it clarifies the color, texture and line of my story. So stories are created, woven together not chronologically but magically to strengthen the connection to the ancestors, the family and the earth. The story I am weaving for Wind in the Mountains and for her granddaughter pulls in many worlds, and the women from those worlds have chosen to be part of it. I am still unpeeling the layers of meaning in Grandmother Mabel's words. Each remembering reveals fuller meaning and enriches the legacy of my family.

Life offered many opportunities for me to redefine this "going/coming back being" I was becoming. What began in the gorge with a name on the wind carried me across this country and down into the southern hemisphere. It brought me new relationships, strengthened old ones, and extended the notion of who my people are to include the Maori of Aotearoa (New Zealand). Like many unwitting adventurers I sometimes did not recognize the purpose of the journey until it was over.

I had been summoned to Aotearoa in 1992 to return a gift of jade, but what I found when I visited there in 1993 and 1994 had very little to do with that. There I saw views of myself that could not be seen in my own land. In that upside-down world I was called to define myself in clarity and detail. I was asked to describe the multiplicity of myself and my thinking from a place of unshakable knowing. It was not a direct question which brought me to this but the mirror of my Maori friends—their self-determined cultural connection to land and ancestors. I had not been aware of the dance I had choreographed inside myself to accommodate the seemingly conflicting memories flowing in my veins from my own diverse ancestors. I had made sense and order of my Scand/African/Lakota heritage, as some of my friends called it. But what I now saw as my heritage was a spiral of almost imperceptible openings. I had formed an apparently seamless multifaceted persona to present to those whom I encountered. In Aotearoa I began to see what it had cost me internally. I had not truly known what the words of my grandmother meant until this going and coming back to myself. What I would experience in a circle of women in Otaki, a town in New Zealand, began in New Mexico the summer of my granddaughter's birth.

That summer I began to connect with people. The winter came, and I still spent time with the land, but I began thinking of new ways to earn a living. The desert made me long to fly, and dancing was the closest thing to flying I could imagine. I began teaching African dance wherever I could find students and space. By accident I came across a few drummers familiar with African dance rhythms. I met Stephen first in another dance class, and he and I began to work together setting up workshops and classes. At one of our classes Stuart walked in with a *djembe*, a wonderful African drum, and just began playing it. It was the kind of forceful drumming I had missed. So the two of them worked with me and helped me connect with other dancers.

At one of the workshops organized for me in Santa Fe, I met Yvette, the wife of Blue Spruce from the Taos pueblo. She was black Seminole and longed for some way to connect to Yoruba ancestry, which was a remembered part of her family history. Looking at her brown skin, green eyes and curly hair, I wondered what else was in the mix, but it never came out in our discoveries of each other. She had grown up as a Seminole with a grandmother who insisted upon claiming her Yoruba heritage and teaching Yvette songs and rituals. There were so many similarities in our lives that we could not spend enough time together wandering in the mountains and exploring what it meant to be a black Indian. It was the first time either of us had met someone else from inside that world.

She asked Blue Spruce to petition the council for permission to teach the dances on their land at the pueblo. I do not know what he said to persuade them, but permission came in the spring, and the dances began under Taos Mountain. Yvette and I, on our hands and knees, cleared sage and cactus and made a space. Guarding the dance circle was a tree which had been split by lightning; at the base of it we made an altar to the spirits of the land, thanking them for bringing us together.

It was a strange thing to be dancing under Taos Mountain calling in African deities. The movements of shoulders and hips to polyrhythmic drumming brought a new kind of energy to this landscape. During the first month, some of the elders would come and sit on a small hill overlooking the dance circle. The first time we danced there, one of them sent a message: "Can you handle what you call up?" I nodded to the elders and invited them to come for the honoring of the land, the drums and the ancestors. A few of them accepted and came the next time we met. They watched intently as we gave smoke and libations. The ritual protocol seemed to put them at ease, and after a month or so they stopped coming. We danced in our bare feet twice a week all through the summer, strong dances on that land. I made very little money, but life kept moving and the joy we all found in praying with the movement of our bodies was its own wealth.

I stayed in contact with my friends on the East Coast, including New York, to make sure I wasn't missing anything, although I was unsure of what that might mean. In May 1990 my friend Tom arrived from Baltimore to have a show in one of the Santa Fe galleries and invited me to the opening party. He was concerned that I had distanced myself from the art world and wanted to help me reconnect.

The party was in a beautiful adobe house near the opera and was crowded with people I didn't know. Everyone was occupied with meeting new people, and I made myself at home next to the only other brown-skinned person in the room. At first glance I thought she was aboriginal or North African, but whatever her ancestry was became unimportant when she smiled. Her entire heart was visible in that smile. She introduced herself as Gail, and we started an all-night conversation that changed my life. Gail had gone to art school with Tom and just happened to be in Santa Fe for his opening. She had been teaching art at university level for years and was now teaching design in an interdisciplinary program at Miami University in Ohio. She was full of life and laughter; I imagined her students to be very lucky.

We shared stories of our lives, our art, our children and our dreams. The party came to an end, and we were still deep in our sharing; when it became clear that the hosts wished to retire, we stood outside to finish our meeting properly. As she said good-bye, she invited me to come to Ohio and teach at Miami University with her. My "yes" began a lightning-speed journey which continues to this moment. I danced the rest of the summer in thanksgiving for this new opening in my life. Gail worked her way through university channels to negotiate the position for me.

In the fall I packed my truck with my belongings, put a few things in storage and headed for Ohio. I entered academia naive, enthusiastic and feeling very rich with my new job. I was called an Academic Challenge Scholar and would be doing what I had done in one form or another for years—teaching my own creative process. The course, Ritual Traditions, was the fine arts component of the first-year interdisciplinary program. I was excited at the chance to work with college students for an entire semester. I had done many short workshops at colleges and universities but had never had the opportunity to work consistently with students over a period of time.

We met twice a week as an art studio, but it turned out that the students and I had come to the act of making with different understandings of the nature of art and of the classroom's role. I came with all of myself. I shared the things I had learned from my elders and my own experience as a maker. I saw the studio as a sacred space and tried to find out what was sacred to the students. I shared from the place that I knew, a place that had no word for art, where making and living are expressions of the same energy and there are no perfectly defined boundaries.

We explored visual identity through the study and making of talismans, shields and altars. I saw these things as a way of identifying the self in relationship to Self, community and the unknown. I saw an opportunity to share what I knew while discovering who the students were. I asked each one to bring what I had brought to the process— the whole self. I didn't know that I was asking something unusual and risky. By the middle of the semester the aggressive tone of some of the students warned me that they did not think this class was school as usual. There had been no place of initiation or rite of passage in their lives to prepare them for evaluation by a community. So the idea of any kind of benevolent judgment based on collaboration and connection was foreign to them, students and faculty alike.

There were many clashes during that semester and many tears, my own and theirs. The language of curriculum and the nature of the work I had set before us could not find a meeting place. The cultural contact zone between our two ways of thinking was a no-man's-land that we could not traverse. I needed new language and new tools if I was to be able to connect my world to this one. Slowly I began to understand the language of the academy and the difference between that way of thinking and my own. I wrote about it to clean my heart and soul. I promised that, if I were ever asked to do it again, I would measure the differences and try to make paths between them to spare us all the pain of contact. I went back to New Mexico thinking I would not see Oxford or Miami again.

It was after that semester that I made my way to Wounded Knee for the memorial. I needed to reconnect to that which had formed me and given me the thoughts and feelings so different from those I had just experienced. The trip brought many memories, strands of other stories, but it also cleared my path so that I could move forward with open eyes.

At the Lost Bird ceremony at Wounded Knee I met an old grandmother whose name I didn't know. I was watching the giveaway and had just given the last of my blankets to someone on stage at the gym when she sat down beside me and took my hand. She held it for a few minutes, looking at me, then said, "You have to give until it hurts." I had given many blankets and gifts and thought that she was criticizing me. But she patted my hand with great affection and wandered off.

I thought about it while I was driving and promised myself that I would send a box of winter clothing back when I got to New Mexico. I had saved most of the money I made in Ohio and bought myself a small trailer. It had been my idea to use the job to become more independent, and a portable home seemed a good first step. When I left Wounded Knee, I hitched it to my truck and started the trip back to New Mexico.

The sight of my new home in the rearview mirror made me drive very carefully. When I reached Amarillo, Texas, I could feel the pull of the desert. It was beginning to sleet, but I was driving below the speed limit in the slow lane, so I went on. I wasn't tired and decided to drive on to Tucumcari and spend the night in New Mexico. Trucks were slowing down, but cars were still driving at normal speeds. Since it was dark I couldn't clearly see the condition of the road. I had just passed through Silverado when I noticed that the road was much icier and that cars had slowed to 35 m. p. h. I slowed down, too, worried about the trailer.

I was trying to figure out which way you steer during a skid with a trailer when I felt a crosswind push against the truck. Before I could think anything else, the truck was skidding sideways across the freeway and over the grass. I knew I would overturn at any minute and that I would die. The truck kept skidding across the access road and finally stopped next to a fence. I was four lanes, a median and an access road away from where I had been. I blinked and looked around; the truck was still upright. Getting out, I saw that there was a flat tire. Then I realized that the trailer was gone. A trail of debris stretched the entire distance I had skidded. The trailer had disintegrated, leaving a pile that was everything I owned in the world.

The road was black ice; cars were skidding off everywhere. I got a flashlight and went to try to get help on the main road. A couple stopped, but by then the state police had arrived. They gave me a ticket for unsafe driving and called for a bulldozer to clear the road. I was still standing in the road looking at all of my things scattered everywhere when the bulldozer arrived. As it pushed the pile into a ditch by the access road, I wandered through the debris and found my *canupa*, my pipe, still intact. It had skidded so far that the pipe bag was shredded away from it. On either side of the road near it were the two halves of my eagle feather. I knew it had saved my life. Remembering the old woman at Wounded Knee, I went back to the truck, got tobacco, and spread it over the rest of the wreckage as my giveaway in thanksgiving for my life. I knew what it meant to give till it hurt.

The bulldozer called a tow truck. I asked if they could fix the flat rather than towing me to the garage, and they agreed. I found a motel in Silverado with a vacancy and checked in. The blank TV gave me somewhere to focus as I tried to calm myself, mourning my losses. I switched on the set to look at the weather, then phoned Gail to let her know what had happened. All night I thought about my near death a few years ago and wondered why I kept finding myself at the edge of life. In that half-sleeping state I could feel the shell around my heart begin to crack and release old pain. I had room in my heart for starting over. My body shook with sobs but there were no tears. I wrapped myself in more blankets and waited for daylight. I didn't know where to go. South Dakota crossed my mind, but I had completed that journey for now. It was New Mexico that called me. I got up with first light and headed for Ojo Caliente and friends.

Kip, who owned the gift shop at the Mineral Springs Hotel, had helped me out many times during my stay in New Mexico, giving advice and connecting me with other people. Always quick to be the first in the community to offer assistance when it was needed, he offered to let me stay in his room at the hotel while I tried to sort out what had happened. I was too numb to protest. I spoke to Gail several times, since she provided continuity for me. We had shopped for the trailer together and talked about my dream of independence with my portable home. She told the other faculty what had happened, and they began a fund for a new trailer. Such an act of kindness after so much dissonance humbled me. I began looking for a place to rent, thinking that whatever gift arrived would help me find an apartment or house. Three weeks later I received enough money to buy a sixteen-foot Airstream. Forty-four people had contributed, sending not only money but also boxes of sheets, towels, dishes and other household necessities. My dream had come true again.

Kip drove me to Albuquerque to buy the Airstream. It took only two hours to find the right one. The moment I saw it I was reminded of my stay with Elmore and Tante Inez. I knew it would be a good home. It was delivered to Ojo Caliente where I had arranged for a hook-up site right by the river on the grounds of the mineral springs. Now that I had my portable home, I had to find out what to do. Still my patron, Kip hired me to work in his gift shop at the hotel. It kept food in my mouth and made me interact with the outside world, since I had begun to fall into my pattern of seclusion and solitude. I also began to work on an essay about my semester at Miami.

There were many emotional knots I tried to unravel as I wrote. Now that I had some distance, I could examine my own emotional turmoil as well as that of the students and other faculty. The writing allowed me to find compassion for all of us; it healed my hurt and opened doors that would help me think about other ways of teaching and learning. I was finding in myself a new voice, that of a mixed blood trying to articulate some of what I had felt and seen. The joy I felt in teaching always had as its shadow the fact that there was no room for the way I had been taught by Grandmother Mabel and Tante Inez. I wondered if I could make a way for that kind of teaching and still remain within the academic framework. In that setting would it be necessary for me to leave some of myself behind when I walked into the classroom? Which part would that be?

Spring brought a sense of beginning and new ideas about sharing knowledge. In my search for something to do next, I spent a lot of time talking to Tod, who was alternately my friend, counselor and fellow artist. We had both arrived in New Mexico around the same time and had met at the Santa Fe fleamarket in our search for ways to earn a living and feed our souls. We shared a need to create something beyond what we saw, and out of that need we began Hummingbird, a learning center.

Tod had been living at the Mineral Springs Hotel as night manager, and by the time we started forming the idea he was ready to move on. I was happy in my trailer looking for a new life. We talked to people we knew and explored all of the abandoned buildings in town searching for a home for our idea. We found an old building on the hill overlooking Ojo which seemed perfect. There was a hole in the roof and no windows or doors, but it did have a circle in the middle of the floor, and the problems seemed minor as we negotiated a rent we could both afford. We spent a month renovating the space and moving my trailer to the hill. We received encouragement and support from the community, from the friends and teachers we wished to invite.

As the place took shape, we wondered why we were doing this, why fate had brought the two of us together for this project. When the work got too hard, we relied on the mantra "If we build it, they will come." And so we kept dreaming and working. The location was perfect for the kind of work we envisioned. It was out of the way enough to offer a feeling of privacy, and there was at least an acre of open land for ceremonies. It was blessed in early spring by a Lakota friend and pipe carrier, Nightchase. We built it and people did come.

Tod and I were not quite sure what drew us together so strongly. We were as different as two people could be in upbringing, education and theology, but somewhere at the heart of things it was clear that we were going in the same direction and were guided by the same influences. His white suburban Virginia upbringing and art school education were far removed from my multiracial, multilingual, nomadic experiences, yet we found a place of joining. Even in our temperaments we covered the range. I was direct and always in motion, and Tod was like a calm and easy stroll on the beach. The differences helped the work get done in many new ways and allowed us to begin Hummingbird as a crossroads for cultures, people and ideas. The summer was filled with workshops on shamanism, dreams, personal growth, dancing, drumming and the teachings from elders of many traditions. People seemed to find our door whenever they were in the area.

I lived in my trailer, and Tod moved into the back half of the building. It gave us both living space for the same amount of rent, and there was plenty of room for workshops, big meals and unexpected overnight guests. We offered free art classes to children in the community and extended an open invitation to elders passing through to come and rest with us. There were no arguments between us, and we attributed the effortlessness to our friendship and to our mutual surrender to whatever happened. As more and more people heard about Hummingbird and visited us, I wished that Denise and the children could be part of the sharing. We spoke fairly often, but their lives were full in Cleveland. We were both busy, and conversations were like catch-up notes.

In the middle of the summer I received word from Gail that I had been invited back for the fall semester to teach the same course as before. I couldn't believe they would even consider having me again, but I was interested in giving it another try. We began to redesign the course over the phone, incorporating much of what we had learned from the past year. I was no longer so naive and did not want to pay the emotional price of my last experience. So I decided to make it a more traditional art course dealing with principles of design. I would bring in artifacts from African and Native American cultures as examples of other models of making art but would not try to reveal the source of their inspiration (or my own, for that matter).

The summer was extremely hectic, and neither Tod nor I had much time for our own personal art. My leaving for Oxford gave us the opportunity to let Hummingbird sleep for a season. Tod could get back to painting, and I could try to learn from my students what and how to teach. I had agreed to stay in an apartment in the residence hall rather than living with Gail, which meant that I might get to know the students better.

Since the wreck I had been nervous about long-distance driving, but in August I made my way through Texas without mishap. I stopped at the site of the wreck and said a prayer of thanksgiving for all the gifts and blessings I had received because of the space created by that loss. The landscape in Texas and Oklahoma was dear to me. Even Arkansas had enough open sky so that I did not feel enclosed. But when I crossed the Mississippi River I always felt a sadness. I was not sure whether it was my own longing for the open grasslands and high deserts or whether it was the land itself which seemed mournful. I did know that the closer I came to Ohio and the denser the vegetation got, the more I began to feel as if I were walking through syrup. The August humidity didn't help the situation.

What I also felt as I crossed the country that year and in the succeeding ones was that, when I moved in the high desert of New Mexico, I was juxtaposing the rhythms of that landscape with my own internal African rhythms. And when I moved across the country and crossed into Arkansas, Tennessee and Ohio I was drawn into the mystery of Selu, the Corn Mother, and the connection to the land of my Lakota ancestors and the first peoples of this land. I was not shifting cultures so much as discovering different resonances within myself which seemed attuned to place and sky.

During this drive I realized that there was also a difference in how I was perceived in these places. In New Mexico I was a teacher of African dances; my connection to Africa and to the spiritual traditions of Central and West Africa was what others acknowledged. But in Ohio I was thought of as a member of the Native American community. It was not that I left Africa behind when I was in Ohio or the Black Hills and my Lakota heritage behind when I was in New Mexico. Each influence was present in a different way wherever I went, but during this drive I became aware of the subtle shift that occurred as I moved across the country. It was like observing my hand and turning it over slowly, so that at one moment I am looking at the top and the next at the palm. It is the same hand, but its characteristics are different from front to back.

The apartment in the residence hall had belonged to the founder of the women's college that had been the previous incarnation of these buildings. It had fourteen-foot ceilings and was bigger than Hummingbird. I moved in, wondering how I would fill the space or reduce it to a comfortable scale. I draped the formal furniture in fabrics and found ways to make it mine temporarily. I kept to myself, shy about the furor I had created the year before. The semester progressed without incident. This course did not have the passion of the previous one, but it cost us all much less. I was relieved at the peacefulness of it but disturbed by how little it reflected my own understanding of art.

In the middle of the term an idea emerged from a conversation with another professor about a class for the second semester on the nature of assimilation. It would be an opportunity for me to design a course around traditional teaching methods and to see how the students would adjust to a nonwestern perspective. I was excited to have a chance to see how the students and the institution would respond to a totally different way of teaching and learning. I wanted to invite elders to teach, but I also wanted to have others come and act as bridges between the elders and the students, to interpret, when necessary, in matters of protocol, language and ideology. I knew many mixed bloods had walked the territory between tradition in Indian Country and the modern world, developing an understanding and language for negotiating this no-man's-land between cultures. Carolyn worked in public health addressing the needs of the native community, and Steve had been teaching Native American cosmology in colleges. They had spent time both with native elders and in the academic environment. They would be with the class for most of the semester, while the elders would be in residence for two or three weeks. It took the rest of the semester to raise the funds to bring everyone and find accommodations for them, but by Christmas the course was in place for the spring and I was able to go back to Hummingbird for a break.

Tod was happy to continue painting while Hummingbird slept, and winter was a good time for him to concentrate on his work. He kept the home fires burning while I prepared for my first social sciences course. I was focusing the course on the Lakota and Bakongo (Central Africa) cultures, using their social structures as the organizing principle. There was much discussion among the students about the inclusion of dances and ceremonies in a course at a state university. They argued that religion and academics were being merged. We had an open forum in which other professors described how, in many indigenous cultures, it is impossible to separate belief, language, and social structure. The murmur of dissent continued, but I was not asked to change the design of the course.

It was in these discussions that I began to experience yet another facet of myself emerging. If I were categorical I would call it my European heritage. It presented itself as an increasing ability to analyze and objectify in order to clarify and impart my own knowledge to the outside world. Much time would pass before I would know what this might mean, but I was enjoying the feeling of being stretched intellectually.

The course began in January of 1992, the year of rediscovery. Students were seeing the origin myth of America deconstructed. Throughout the world of education ran the theme of seeing history with others' eyes. Instead of bombarding the students with information, I opened my apartment to them. Now the huge rooms were barely large enough. Meals were open to anyone who happened to be there. Both Wallace Black Elk and Dr. Bunseki Fu-Kiau, the elders I had invited, did most of their teaching in my living room. The students came during class time, or whenever they were free, to sit and listen and help prepare food. They learned the protocol of caring for elders and of respectful listening. Sweatlodge, moonlodge and dance ceremonies were held regularly, and students learned to help the visitors prepare for these. There was a lot of physical work, which was unusual for a college course, but everyone seemed eager to have something real to do. We built the sweatlodge in the woods behind the residence hall, well hidden from the rest of the campus so it would not be an object of curiosity.

Listening to Wallace speak about Lakota beliefs and Fu-Kiau talk about Bakongo cosmology confirmed what I had known in my heart all along. They were talking about the same Great Mystery. There were many similarities and crossovers in their teachings; listening to either of them, I would find the essence of what I had learned from Grandmother Mabel, from Tante Inez, from all the beings on earth when I took the time to hear. The earth does not ask me to choose one or the other of these ways but reminds me of all the teachings each sunrise and sunset and with each flight of the hawk. These teachings came together naturally in the trees and the sky and the earth, and I found great strength in seeing them connected, as well as shining separately, in the voices of these elders.

As spring approached we were beginning to feel like family. There was a strong core of students who had spent as much time as possible working with the elders and other visitors. There were also those who viewed the course as just another class and gave it the allotted time, nothing more.

I took a break in March, having accepted an invitation to an indigenous people's conference in Eugene, Oregon. I had been asked to participate in the opening and closing ceremonies and was honored, though a little bewildered. I left knowing that learning would continue whether I was at school or not. The apartment remained open during my absence as a place for students to gather and talk.

The woman who met me at the airport gave a face to the voice I had been hearing on the phone for months. She took me to my lodgings and gave instructions for the ceremonies that would take place the following day. In the material about the conference, I had seen that we were all expected to come to the opening in regalia. What kind I would wear to represent my mixed blood was an interesting question; I had decided to dress in the white of the ancestors and was to be introduced as Lakota/Bantu. I had brought words from Fu-Kiau in Kikongo, his native language, as my greeting since I knew there would be no other African presence at the conference. I was sorry that he had not been invited but his words brought him with me.

In the morning as we stood like exhibitions for an indigenous museum, my eyes rested on a small delegation, the members of which resembled huge birds inside an enclosure. With their long feather cloaks, they seemed like relatives from some past I could not quite remember. They were smiling at me, and I found myself rushing towards them. A young woman reached her arms out in greeting like a sister; behind her was her mother and a man who was clearly an elder. With outstretched arms and smiles, we met in the center of the hall. I discovered that they were the Maori delegation from New Zealand. Already others in the hall had been drawn to our meeting, as if they were watching a long-separated family reunite. We didn't introduce ourselves right away. We kept smiling and remarking at how familiar we looked and felt to each other. Hema and I decided we were truly sisters, and her mother, Dell Wihongi, agreed. TePere, regal with his feather cloak and staff, introduced himself and suggested we meet in their room after the opening. The hall quieted, and we could feel ourselves guided towards the door. The opening prayer had already begun.

We had entered as a family but were separated by our introductions. Each of us prayed and addressed the gathering. We stood together in a circle afterwards and said private prayers acknowledging the gifts each had brought. As I gave my small pouch to TePere he placed it in the pocket over his heart and covered it with his hand. Quietly he asked me to come see him afterward.

The prayers, invocations, introductions and speeches lasted most of the morning, but at the first break I went to TePere's room. Dell, Hema and TePere were relaxing before the afternoon's panels. He began right away to tell me that he had seen me at the fire ceremony that morning and remembered that I had said that I was teaching somewhere in Iowa or Idaho or Ohio. I told him that I had overslept and missed the fire ceremony, and that he must have mistaken someone else for me.

He smiled. "No, we met this morning. I knew you would be here." I was trying to figure out what he meant as he left for a drink of water. Hema and Dell laughed and we jumped on the bed, stories tumbling out and filling the room.

I spent most of my free time between panels and discussion groups with Hema and TePere, laughing, talking and learning about New Zealand. The three days of the conference went much too quickly, and on the last day we gathered again for the closing. Dell spoke first. Her words were visionary and called on us to look to the future from the shoulders of our ancestors. Her words came from strength, not blame, and it brought the room to silence. I was carried back to Shiprock and the power of the feminine I had experienced there. She gave voice to that power.

When she came off the stage, I needed to pay tribute to such a powerful female presence. She seemed to be the voice of the future, her words coming from a place of clarity and assurance. I took from around my neck a carving Tante Inez had given me and handed it to her. The piece was an acknowledgment of what Dell had brought to me as an individual woman as well as to this gathering. I was to speak next, and so we smiled at each other, moving in opposite directions. Since no words seemed adequate to follow her, I sang a song for Elegua, keeper of the crossroads. It seemed to me that we were at a crossroads, and I was singing so that we might choose to follow the strength in Dell's words.

As everyone headed for the lobby, I went to look for Dell and Hema. I found them looking for me, too. Dell was wearing the carving. She took Hema's hand and mine and led us to a quiet spot. She said she had something to give me in return for my gift of love and support. She took a large jade carving from Hema's neck and placed it around mine.

"I cannot give you the jade that I am wearing because it is a symbol of my place in my tribe. So I give this greenstone to you so that you can bring it back to us. When you return it we will have one carved to replace it. This has been handed down through the women in our family for generations, and we ask you to care for it and have a safe journey bringing it back to us. It will make the way for you to come to us."

I was shocked not only by the giving but by the mandate to bring it back to them in New Zealand. I had never even thought of going there. Just as I was trying to recover from my tears and speechlessness, TePere arrived. He had been looking for me when he made his closing address, which had included a presentation of the three baskets of knowledge to three women as keepers of the future. He had given one to a Navajo woman and one to a woman from Brazil, and then he had called my name from the podium. He held out the basket to me. This in addition to the jade around my neck brought more tears. There were no words to respond to such an honor.

We had only an hour until departure time. A woman in the lobby offered to take our photograph. Thinking that we were long-lost family, she offered to finish the roll and give it to us or send us the photos, so we gave her our addresses. We decided to go outside for the photograph, realizing that it was the first time we had been outdoors since the beginning of the conference. We all laughed at how strange it was to have a conference for indigenous peoples in a climate-controlled hotel environment! We exchanged addresses, and TePere told me that he and Dell would make certain that I found my way to all of the people who would teach me. They were so certain of my going there to return the jade that I also began to believe it.

I went back to school feeling overwhelmed and exhilarated. I had never had such a strong and open relationship with anyone. It was as if they understood who I was, with all of my facets, and accepted me. I wore the jade near my skin to absorb the power of the women who had worn it for generations. It was carved in the shape of a hook, and a small piece was chipped off near the tip. I had been told that it happened when one of the grandchildren who was teething on it dropped it. There was so much living entrusted to my care.

We were having sweatlodge at least twice a week with the students, and I wore it in the lodge every time. The connection between the hemispheres began to become almost visible to me. Every time someone asked about the jade, I told the story, explaining that I was meant to go to New Zealand. I wasn't sure how I would get there, but I felt that the trip was coming nearer. Every time I touched the pendant I became more certain. It was just the "how" that eluded me.

As the semester wound to a close, my apartment continued to be the hub of a small emerging community. Both Wallace Black Elk and Dr. Bunseki Fu-Kiau had brought the students and other faculty into contact with whole new ways of teaching and thinking. There was excitement and some resentment. The class, being concerned with opening new perceptions and also offering students the option of being with elders and teachers, seemed to spread throughout the department, taking more than its allotted share of time. I had made an attempt to collaborate with other teachers and share resources so the situation would not become competive, but the boundaries between courses turned out to be much more static than I had imagined.

Right before the end of the semester, as everyone was spending time outdoors to enjoy spring's smells and the return of sunlight, I received an invitation to go to New York and give a talk and performance about black Indians, in history and in the present. I did not like to leave so close to the end of the class, but it was a great opportunity to see old friends and get a good dose of urban adrenaline before settling back into the rhythm of the high desert.

As if I were returning to the place of my childhood, I found my way to all of the street corners, restaurants and shops that formed the map of my memory of the city. Most of my life there had been confined to Harlem or Soho and the East Village. Walking the streets was like calling up faces from my scrapbook. I seemed to run into everyone I had known. Being back in a world where there were more art openings than one could attend in an evening was a treat I had missed. As I walked into my fourth or fifth opening, I ran into a friend I had not seen in years. Dorothy had been an intern with my first gallery, and now she was working for a private foundation. She was in a hurry but pleased to see me. We chatted briefly; then, as she was leaving, she held something out to me.

"I know there is somewhere you want to go. Apply for this grant. Call me."

She gave me her business card from the Lila Wallace Foundation, and I put it in my pocket, feeling like everything else had become background. I touched the jade pendant with more than a little awe at its power. I phoned Tod that evening to tell him about my brief meeting with Dorothy and to hear what he thought. (I had told him the story of my meeting with the Maori in installments, from Eugene and from Oxford.) He was as certain as I that the trip would happen. I kept feeling as if I were careening toward some new dimension, with no say about the direction it would take. As always he offered good counsel and reminded me that even in falling there was an effortless flow of grace. It sounded so simple when he said it. But I remembered hearing once that "it's simple. It's just not easy."

I was happy to be heading back to Hummingbird even though I was secure in the knowledge that Tod had been keeping the spirit of the place alive and well. I had already decided that it would be helpful for us to invite Fu-Kiau there so that we might have the benefit of the kind of teaching the students had enjoyed. I was sure there were many in New Mexico who would be able to learn from him. Tod and I resettled into our roles as the caretakers of Hummingbird, finding it easier than ever to accommodate the flow of visitors and seekers and feeling a deepening of our own friendship.

I procrastinated about the application, rationalizing that I needed a vacation after teaching for a full year. Then I delved into the mechanics of grant writing, sponsorship and recommendations. I decided to apply for a trip to New Zealand, where I would learn about the Maoris' use of visual imagery for recording history; then I would return to Ohio to do a large earth sculpture in honor of the native people who had been removed from the landscape. I found support for the earth work through the Women's Center at Miami, and I wrote to Dell and Hema in New Zealand and asked for an official invitation to include with the grant. They responded by return mail, and the grant went into the decision pool as summer came to the high desert of New Mexico.

Gail, Terry and I had decided to combine our passions and teach a summer studio in New Mexico for Miami. (Terry was a friend who had gone with me to Wounded Knee, and whom I had made my brother according to the Lakota tradition of *hunkayapi*, the making of relatives the next year.) As students arrived for the course, Tod and I had to find new ways to protect our fragile private lives from the daily activity of twenty-year-olds acclimating to life without the accustomed comforts. We no longer thought it difficult or strange to live twenty to thirty miles from the nearest grocery store or fast food restaurant. But to students from suburban Ohio, the accommodations and the town of Ojo itself seemed like a leap backward into some primitive lifestyle, accompanied by the plague of endless sky. We planned field trips so they could stop at McDonald's; this gave them a sense of security and also presented some diversity in the landscape.

Terry and I were reminded of our trip to Wounded Knee and how we had felt comforted as the sky opened and the views extended. But we had memories of the plains landscape from our childhoods and knew that the browns and silvers of the grasslands hold many secrets. We tried to remain compassionate but could not hide our pleasure at the distance from amenities. It was Gail with her endless patience and smiles who made the bridge between our enthusiasm and the relentless sky and sun.

Fu-Kiau's visit followed the workshop so closely that I didn't notice the break. His presence brought more visitors and shed new light on the confluence of my Lakota and African worlds. I wondered who would come to hear his teachings and was surprised when a local Hispanic family came with gifts to ask for a healing for their daughter. But I was even more pleased when a Lakota friend of mine came with her family to listen and to share with us. We sat for hours asking questions of each other on matters of ritual and essential beliefs and found ourselves reeling in the swelling spiral of convergence.

In the midst of this I watched Tod open and stretch to share this place with us, offering his own faith to the journey. I realized that I had been living with the person of my search. For the first time I saw the poetry in his soul, what I had been looking for since I was a child. I was suddenly pulled into his brown eyes and into the light of his spirit. He had always been handsome and charming, but now there was an extra dimension that made me recognize something I had not seen in him before. We had been true friends and partners, and it had never occurred to either of us to look beyond that.

A few days after Fu-Kiau's departure, we moved from being room-mates to live-in lovers with such ease that it astonished both of us. There was no transition and no need to play any of the romantic games of deception. We knew each other too well. So we stepped into life as a couple standing on the foundation of a deep friendship. Once our friends realized the change they said they had known it all along. I wondered why we had not been aware of it. I was still too uncertain about being in a relationship to realize how unique ours was among our friends. We had seen each other at the worst of times and the best of times, so we simply continued to live truthfully with each other, doubts and all.

My appointment at Miami was renewed for the following fall, but I was moved to a new department. As the summer drew to a close, Tod and I were uncertain as to how the separation would affect our new relationship. Although for years I had been the traveler and Tod the keeper of the hearth, this was a new test. We needn't have worried. The dynamics stayed the same. I did feel less adrift at school and made an effort to get back home at least once during the semester. I didn't say much to Denise about Tod, but we talked often, and she knew that there was someone. I was busy weaving a new chapter in my life, and it was too fragile and incomplete to be revealed.

In the background of my thoughts I was waiting. I received several letters from Hema and Dell, and every time I wore the pendant I could feel the call of that lineage of women. I returned to Grandmother Mabel's teachings and to the moonlodge, a circle of women friends and colleagues who got together at each full moon. We didn't build a moonlodge structure but found form in our gathering to sit with the full moon. There were five or six women who came when they could. We all came from different cultural and spiritual backgrounds, and we found commonality in the giving of time to our bodies and the thirteen cycles of the moon. Each of us brought memories and dreams to the circle. We found joy and strength in the synchronization of our cycles and in the silence we shared. I was teaching and working at my relationship with Tod long distance, but the moonlodge became the focus of that time in Ohio.

Many times we were able to sit only for an hour or two because of our commitments to family and work. But we had promised ourselves to sit one whole moon together. In October we finally made the time and decided to sit in a field which belonged to one of the women. It was cold, so we gathered blankets and sleeping bags for our all-night vigil. We added more candles than usual to the altar to give a sense of warmth. By sunset we were settled in silence. We could see the rim of the hill where the moon would rise. We sat wrapped in our sleeping bags, our bodies touching, staring through the candlelight to the darkness beyond, waiting for the grand entrance of the moon. Determined not to fall asleep, we huddled closely together, not so much from the cold as in a spirit of resolve.

The cold night had other things in mind, and soon we were lying spoon fashion in our blankets and bags, watching the dancing shadows made from moonlight and candlelight. The moon had insinuated herself over the rim of the hill and flooded our circle with her presence. I felt pressed into my blankets by forces I couldn't see. Searching for shapes in the shadows, I drifted into half sleep. Then I was awakened, choked by a feeling which I could not describe or contain. I felt stifled, as if the air were being drained by the presence of so many beings. The night was only half over. I sat up, thinking that might help me gain control over what was happening. Everyone else was quiet, and I could only imagine that their dreams were filled with the same feeling.

I called on Grandmother Mabel to help and guide me and to forgive me if I had done something inappropriate in the lodge. Trying to calm down by listening to my own breath, I waited to hear the quietness of her voice in my heart. Even when she was alive it had always been a surprise to see that she could command such attention with a voice so sweet and soft.

In the quiet we can hear our heart. The edges have a lot of questions. Sometimes they break the quiet. We can't hear the moon when we break the quiet. But you can feel the questions pushin' in. We gotta make room for the answers in our heart.

There was the smell of sweetgrass; the shadows found their place back in the night. My lungs expanded, and I began to see the ways in which we let questions cut off the ties between the grandmothers' voices and our bodies' cycles. When we are quiet and still, the crimson tides of our bodies speak to us and in their whispers are our answers. I fell asleep, hoping the others had found their grandmothers, too.

As the sun began to rise we stood wordlessly to watch it overtake the sky. We broke the silence and our fast, greeting the morning with food and singing.

We went back to our lives with the stillness inside us, marvelling that something so simple could bring us such peace. By the next full moon, we were ready before sunset. From sunset to moonrise we sang and drummed our invitation to the moon and the grandmothers who had walked before us. The music came from many cultures—Lakota songs, African songs, gospel songs and children's songs.

The women found ways to make themselves comfortable for the night. We had gathered to find what we had forgotten in our bodies and in our spirits. As the moon rose over the east gate of the lodge (an owl wing placed there to mark the direction) and bathed us in her light, we settled into a silence that would last until sunrise. Everyone began sitting up to focus on the moon. I had burning questions about Tod and New Zealand and my teaching; the internal chatter of these questions continued into the moonlit night. I could feel the ground under me as a presence, could smell the cedar that had been sprinkled over it. I looked at the water gleaming in the turtle shell that was the center of our circle and at the women beginning to curl into each other. I remembered Grandmother Mabel's words about going and coming back.

I called to the directions to still the chatter, and to the owls to carry me silently on the motion of their wings, and to all the other women on the earth to hold my hand in the stillness. I called to the grandmothers who had walked this road before me to petition the moon to light their footsteps so that I might follow them. I called to my granddaughter and to all the following generations to have the stamina to sit in their own circles and listen to the moon. Finally came the silence—there was nothing more to say or think, only the moon on my body, the cold of the night and the shoulder of the woman next to me touching mine.

After the two all-night lodges, we fell back into the hectic nature of life at the university and met for only a few hours at the full moon.

People had commitments and visitors; the timing was never right, and it was getting much colder. But each time we sat for even an hour, we were called back into the force of the silence we had experienced and its connection through the tides of our bodies to the moon. Other memories of that semester ride on the lodge and are overshadowed by it.

Shortly before the semester ended, Tod phoned to tell me, quite nonchalantly, that I had received a Lila Wallace International Artist Award for my trip to New Zealand. I could hardly believe it. He forwarded the letter to me so that I had tangible proof of my chance to go to New Zealand for six months. In the midst of my excitement, I was also devastated at the thought of being away from him for six more months after a semester of separation. I decided to just sit with the news for a few days and then read all the information and call to find out particulars.

I have never been one for reading instructions or enclosed literature, so I phoned. It was a relief to find out that I could make two trips of three months each and still fulfill the grant. I postponed planning my departure until I got home to New Mexico and Tod and I could talk about it. I wondered if he had any passion for coming along, but it seemed unlikely that he would leave the easel for an adventure of such length.

We talked about my trip and our feelings about changes in the nature of our relationship and our own individual growth. The world we had built in Ojo around perceptions we held of ourselves seemed limited both by our environment and our lifestyle. We wanted to explore new ways of living and new relationships to people and landscape. With each day we came closer to the conclusion that it was time to leave Ojo and perhaps New Mexico. Tod had suggested Washington State, near Seattle, since we had friends there and it would give us a chance to explore a bigger city. I agreed, even though I knew that I would grieve for the desert. So the winter was focused on completing the move before I had to leave for New Zealand. It was not the most prudent piece of timing, but caution had never been part of our lives. I packed in shifts, trying to separate what I would need on my trip from what I would be moving into a new house. It was the kind of routine activity that kept me from feeling overwhelmed at the quantum leap we were taking.

I cried as we left the desert, and I cried many times along the way. It was clear that Tod and I were on a new life adventure. That felt good, but I was leaving the landscape that fed my soul. I consoled myself with the thought that perhaps I would find work there that would allow me to spend more time with Tod. I decided to focus on that possibility when I returned from New Zealand. It was not clear whether I would be returning to Miami. I had taken some pleasure in letting them know that I had received the grant and would not be back for the coming semester. I didn't want to be taken for granted, and it was a good chance to remind them that I was an artist, too. It did, however, bring a level of uncertainty back into my life.

I waited for the trees to close the sky away from my view and the moisture in the air to weigh me down. During the first few days we stayed on the coast, the humidity misted my sight. The way I saw the energy of objects or persons at the same time that I saw them was gone. It was like going temporarily blind. I couldn't imagine the cause, but it felt as if the water in the air obscured the view. I walked among the trees and found the landscape empty of detail and overlay. I couldn't discern the shades of green or the shapes of the individual leaves, because they seemed flat and abstracted. I was slowed down by the effort it took to look out the window. My sight was attuned to the subtleties of the desert, to a silence that allowed the flow of my own blood and heartbeat to be present. Now all views were equal and competed for attention.

For as long as I could remember, I had experienced the world by seeing people and objects come into view surrounded by their fields of energy. I had not known that this was more than ordinary sight until I lost the ability in Washington; I hadn't realized that my way of seeing was unusual. As I started explaining to Tod what was missing, I came to understand that he didn't see that way. What I claimed as natural sight was an extra ingredient to him, something psychically developed. Whatever it was, I felt blind without it, and the world was reduced by one dimension.

We found a house on Puget Sound, which everyone said was lucky. The house was right on the rocky beach. There was a nest of bald eagles very near, and they flew over our deck daily. I felt relieved by their presence. Perhaps they saw in the landscape what I no longer could. Waiting for the reappearance of my way of seeing, I stayed inside most of the time and paid attention to the rhythm Tod and I made as a couple in a real house. I packed again for New Zealand.

My flight was scheduled to leave from Seattle, and I had not received word from Dell or Hema that they would meet me at the airport, so I was very uncertain about what awaited me. Tod was finding a new palette in his painting as a result of the change in scenery and was looking forward to the solitude with its creative juices. Even though our friends found it strange, they marveled at how well we managed these lengthy separations, and even thrived on them. Such periods of time allowed us to concentrate fully on our own visions without the interruption of daily relationship maintenance and provided us with great creative bursts as well as a true appreciation of the time we did have together.

It was September and still warm in Seattle, the harbor full of tourists and no hint of the coming chill. Entering the plane, I thought of the months since leaving school and found myself shedding tears, not from sadness but from release. It was giveaway of the same magnitude as that of the wreck in Texas, but the gifts were not my material belongings. The way I had thought things would be was dissolving into the way they really were, and the tears came from the release of old views.

I slept most of the way from Los Angeles, but midway through the trip I was awakened by what seemed like a single bump, as if the plane had hit an obstruction and passed over it. I wondered if you could actually feel the crossing of the equator. Later, having been successfully met at the airport and driven to Dell's home, I remembered that moment. We were sitting in the kitchen, where I was distributing gifts and talking about how strange it felt to lose a day in the sky. I recalled the bump and laughingly told them what I thought I had felt.

Dell was very serious when she spoke. "You have come to the feminine side of the world to make yourself whole, and you entered our protection when you crossed the equator. The bump you felt was your coming into the arms of our love."

As she spoke I noticed that I was seeing all of her, that she and her granddaughters were surrounded by their energy. I looked out the window and saw the same fullness in the trees and plants. It was too much to tell, but I felt it was the presence of those loving arms.

Even surrounded by so much affection and excitement, the first three days were very difficult. I was left alone so that "your soul can catch up with your body," while everyone in the house went about their jobs and lives. Dell and her granddaughters smoked, and there was a small dog in the house as well, so I was concerned about my allergies. Most of all I was disconcerted at my place in the household and in the Maori community as a guest/child/pupil. I was being called upon to surrender to the flow of life as it was presented to me. Many years had passed since I had trusted enough to do that. Now I was being asked to place that trust in strangers, and it was only the presence of their immense love that could make it possible.

I phoned Tod on the third day, trying not to show how out of control I felt. But I have never been able to hide from him, and when he heard my voice he suggested giving back the grant so that I could come home. It was a frivolous and fear-laden thought, but I was comforted to know that such a thing could be considered if I was truly miserable. Just the suggestion of it helped me to come to grips with what was in store for me and begin to see the magic of it.

Wanting to have no preconceived ideas about the place, I had purposely not read anything about the Maori or New Zealand before coming. So, meeting a woman for the first time, I was not prepared for the *hongi* , the traditional greeting of touching nose and forehead. The sharing of breath is such an intimate and trusting act, and it had to happen many times before I lost my feeling of discomfiture.

I had had no idea what the Maori language was like, but everywhere Dell took me I was immersed in it. It seemed as if I could feel and smell the sea in the words. I let it wash over me in waves, and felt as though I could sense the nature of what was being said even if I could not follow the details. Whenever I was called on to speak at a meeting or in a *marae* (meeting house), I sang. People always came up to me afterwards to tell me that without knowing the language they understood the songs.

I sang Lakota songs many times during my stay, as I learned what an important place the sharing of song has in Maori protocol and daily life. I chose these songs because I was being led into the heart of this culture and land and wished to return the gift with something from the land which forged me. On these islands I found myself longing for *Paha Sapa*, the Black Hills, and for the desert of the Southwest. I kept trying to describe those landscapes to a people of rainforest and ocean.

These first three months were filled with the newness of the place and the people and my feeble attempts to learn Maori. I traveled all over both islands under Dell's watchful eye and protection. I was welcomed into countless *maraes* as I became more comfortable with the formalities and with the seeming intimacy of the social structure. TePere also made it possible for me to spend time with his family in Rotorua and to visit the sulfur pools and the cultural center.

I had made no specific plans for the trip but rather had chosen to let it unfold. It was clear that my hosts wanted me to see as much of the country and of the internal bicultural politics as possible. I sat in on many meetings between Maori and government officials. But the joy came in visiting the *Kohanga Reo,* the language nests, where preschool children learn Maori language and culture. It was a good way for me to learn some rudimentary words and songs without embarrassment. I was feeling very much like a child myself.

I began to be able to distinguish the individual nature of the ferns and trees and bushes as I noticed these motifs appearing in Maori carving, painting and weaving. I looked more closely at the carving in the *maraes* I visited. Observing as children wove small baskets, I wished my own hands could participate, but I also understood that just being close, physically and psychically, was a good way to learn. I looked for any opportunity to see weavers and carvers at work.

The train ride to Wellington was my first chance to be silent in months, and, as I watched the countryside move outside the window through the thousands of shades of green, I no longer felt suffocated by the abundance in the landscape. But I was also becoming increasingly aware that I was a child of the plains, and that the verdant nature of this place had clarified my attachment to that landscape beyond any doubt. I could no longer claim that "I could live anywhere"; it was clear that my heart and soul belonged to the grasslands.

In Wellington Hema and I reconnected as sisters, and I was pleased to have the opportunity to return the jade which Dell had removed from her neck. I placed it in her hands, thanking her for giving me the means to get to Aotearoa. But she and Dell had changed their minds—I was to pass it on to my daughter and granddaughter. So she replaced it around my neck. I couldn't believe that they were letting go of so much of their history. Tears came easily for both of us as we acknowledged the truth of our sisterhood.

Hema was sure that there were others with whom I would feel the same kinship, and we headed off the next morning for PakiPaki and a meeting of healers. I looked forward to spending nights at the *marae* and dreaming inside the body of the ancestors.

Upon arrival, we waited outside for a *powhiri*, an official welcome. Then I followed Hema into the meeting house. Several other groups of people were there, picking their sleeping areas from among mattresses side by side down each long wall. In addition to the carved beams and posts and the paintings and weavings, there were photographs of ancestors on all the walls. We were sleeping in the presence and protection of this entire lineage.

Every meal at the *marae* filled my body and my heart. I watched the entire family help prepare and serve the food, and the process seemed flawless. Each time different people were cooking, serving or cleaning, and there did not seem to be an overseer. Jobs got done because they needed doing, not because someone was asked to do them. Watching closely as I helped set the tables or clear the dishes to see how the work was delegated, I could never catch the moment of task-giving or list-making. Everyone seemed attuned to the needs of the *marae* as a mother is to a child and worked effortlessly together.

As we came together the next day for a talking circle, I spoke about the beauty of the way everyone worked at the *marae*. We shared our thoughts about family, clan, tribe and nation. English words do not express the things we spoke about because they are small, flat words. The *whanau, iwi, hapu, waka* of the Maori, the *tiospaye* and *oyate* of the Lakota and the *mbongi* of the Bakongo are words of relationship, time, space and mind. We spoke from our hearts so that we would begin to know one another.

After the talking circle, there were many questions about my own upbringing and cultures. I had spoken of the moonlodge, and the women were anxious to experience one as well as to share some of their own teachings. I did not agree to it immediately, wanting to know where it would be and how the people of that place would feel about it. I also needed to pray about bringing ceremony to a new landscape with different spirits.

As I waited to understand these things, I continued my journey. I finally met a group of weavers who gave my hands the gift of working with *harekeke,* the flax, in a way that helped me to understand its place in Maori life. In many ways it is as important as the buffalo once was in the plains. Its leaves are woven into baskets for fishing and carrying; its fibres are used in making clothes for the weather (rain capes, hats, sandals), rope, and tools and cloaks, which demonstrate power.

The more I learned, the more comfortable I was in the landscape. I became obsessed with the spirals of the *pungau* ferns and looked for them whenever we walked in the forests. I also learned some of the medicinal plants, since the thick, humid atmosphere was hard on my lungs. I loved being busy with my hands, weaving and winding rope, and I was anxious for the chance to try some traditional dyeing methods.

Just as I was beginning to make my way on my own without so much assistance and protection from Dell, my first three months came to an end. I flew home thinking about the bump at the equator but somehow slept through it. I wanted to process some of my experience before being more fully immersed in the Maori culture. During the flight I practiced some of the songs I had learned at the *Kohanga*.

I thought about "grandmothers always singing you going. Grandchildren always singing you coming back. Somebody always singing you, going/coming back being." The songs of my grandmothers had helped me on my journey in Aotearoa, and the songs of the grandchildren were filling my return. As I carried stories lived in various landscapes around the world to different people, I wondered if I was beginning to understand both myself and Grandmother Mabel's words.

Tod and I rejoiced at being together again, but it was not an easy time. We had experienced diametrically opposed kinds of lives during our separation. I had been surrounded by people's loving arms almost every minute since I had left. He had been isolated at the beach house and had barely spoken to anyone else during the three months.

Great patience was required to navigate the gap between us. The difficulty was compounded by the fact that the lifestyle of the beach house seemed so excessive compared to the one I had been living. I had found an indigenous culture which welcomed me without judging me. I had lived simply, in communion with people and the land. It was almost impossible to communicate how restful this had been for me without sounding critical of the life Tod had been leading. We called it the "sandpaper time," and it occurs even now after we have spent an extended time apart.

We found ways to laugh, rediscover our rhythm, and begin to prepare for the next three-month separation. We exchanged gifts, which came from the love we had for each other. He had painted my portrait— the first, I think, he had ever done. I gave him the first basket I had woven in memory of my grandmother. The friction eased, and we both went back to our dreams and our work from the comfort and strength of our relationship. I was excited about my return, because it was already planned for me to have time with several weavers and a man who made stone tools. I would have a chance to visit a master carver, do some traditional bark dyeing on the coast, and see parts of the north island which I had missed on the first trip. I had thought that my return would be about connecting with these things, but when I went back, three weeks later, I found something else waiting for me.

Three days after I felt the bump of the equator, I found myself in Otaki with a group of women preparing for the moonlodge. The light was changing, and everything turned into an outline of itself as the cries of the Maori women echoed across the field. It was the *karanga,* a call to the spirits. Their voices filled the night as they moved toward the moonlodge.

It was autumn in New Zealand, and the night chill had been erased by the power of their voices. As the shadows descended I could see the moonlodge gates and the altar of flowers, ferns and offerings. This was why I had come—to see the moonlodge as part of the hoop of remembrance and to know that it awakened the memory even in another hemisphere and another people. The women in the circle of life were becoming visible one by one as I made my way in life. Each one brought a story or a memory which I carried in my heart.

My life had blossomed in the summer of my granddaughter's birth, but it was not until my trip to Aotearoa that I began to see the nature of our gift. From the moment of Grandmother Mabel's dreaming we began a dance that would encompass many continents and races. As I learned from the Maori in New Zealand and found myself defined in their eyes, I realized that this was a dance between worlds and that I was choreographer, dancer and audience. This knowledge flowed in the blood in my veins and would pass on to my children and their children. I was just beginning to know that I was dancing.